Arduino Computer Vision Programming

Design and develop real-world computer vision applications with the powerful combination of OpenCV and Arduino

Özen Özkaya

Giray Yıllıkçı

[PACKT] open source ✳
PUBLISHING   community experience distilled

BIRMINGHAM - MUMBAI

Arduino Computer Vision Programming

First published: August 2015

Production reference: 1250815

Published by Packt Publishing Ltd.
Livery Place
35 Livery Street
Birmingham B3 2PB, UK.

ISBN 978-1-78355-262-7

www.packtpub.com

Credits

Authors
Özen Özkaya
Giray Yıllıkçı

Reviewers
Avirup Basu
Roberto Gallea
Seyed Mohsen Mousavi
Surya Penmetsa
Randy Schur

Commissioning Editor
Priya Singh

Acquisition Editor
Neha Nagwekar

Content Development Editor
Shweta Pant

Technical Editor
Narsimha Pai

Copy Editors
Dipti Mankame
Kevin McGowan

Project Coordinator
Sanjeet Rao

Proofreader
Safis Editing

Indexer
Priya Sane

Graphics
Sheetal Aute

Production Coordinator
Shantanu N. Zagade

Cover Work
Shantanu N. Zagade

About the Authors

Özen Özkaya is an embedded systems engineer who has been involved in the design, development, and verification of various applications of computer vision and embedded systems for more than 6 years. He strongly believes in the power of sharing knowledge and continuously extending the computer vision.

After earning 6 years of experience in the profession, he is now working for Siemens as a senior development engineer, where he is involved in the research and development of industrial control devices and industrial communication processors. He also contributes to software quality assurance projects in Siemens. He has a total of eight patent applications up to now, and all of his applications are still in progress. He completed a bachelor's program in electronics engineering from İstanbul Technical University (ITU) in 3 years with high honor certificates. He holds a master's degree in electronics engineering from ITU and is currently pursuing a PhD in electronics engineering there. During his academic studies, he worked in various laboratories, such as the medical system design lab, control and avionics lab, robotics lab, pattern recognition and signal processing lab, industrial automation lab, and finally, the embedded systems lab.

In addition to his academic studies, he is now a mentor in the embedded systems laboratory at ITU.

Özen can be reached directly via e-mail at ozenozkaya@gmail.com or contact@ozenozkaya.com. If you want to learn more about him, visit his website at http://www.ozenozkaya.com.

First of all, I would like to thank my parents, Kıyas and Ferah, for their endless effort and perseverance in bringing me up to this level.

My academic advisor, Assoc. Prof. Dr. S. Berna Örs Yalcin, always supported me and helped me achieve many things, so I would like to thank her. I would also like to thank all my friends; the list is too long to mention here.

Above all, a huge special thanks to Nilay Tüfek, who supported me a lot in the writing of this book. She also sincerely encouraged me to accept this challenge and overcome it.

Giray Yıllıkçı is focuses on embedded systems, computer vision, and robotics. He has been contributing to these areas in both the industrial and academic fields. He enjoys sharing his knowledge and experiences of the field with juniors. He believes that sharing information is the true way of proceeding in life.

Giray is currently working as a senior research engineer at Design Lab, Koç University, where he is coordinating the technical process of projects. He is responsible for designing industrial-level proof of concepts for studies at Design Lab. In addition, he manages technical research engineers. His six patent applications are in progress.

He has a bachelor's degree in physics from Koç University. Now, he is currently working on his MS thesis for a graduation program in satellite communication and remote sensing at Istanbul Technical University.

More about him can be found at his website http://www.girayyillikci.com. He can be contacted via gyillikci@gmail.com or gyillikci@ku.edu.tr.

First, I would like to express my gratitude to Özen Özkaya for enabling me to be a part of this book.

I would like to thank the Packt crew who provided support, and offered comments and assistance. At this point, I would like to thank Seyed Mousavi for his valuable reviews and Shweta Pant for successful content development management.

Thank you to Cetin Seren for his guidance in my career. His wise advice and fruitful discussions have led me to achieve the best in my field.

I would like to thank Süreyya Ciliv for providing us with an intellectual and inspiring work environment at Turkcell Technology Applied Research Center, where we received a lot of inspiring know-how.

Thanks to Tugce Pakakar and her friends for helping me enjoy the process of writing this book.

Above all, I am thankful to my mother, father, and brother, who supported, encouraged, and inspired me throughout my life. I would like to express my most sincere gratitude to them with these lines.

About the Reviewers

Avirup Basu is currently a student pursuing a BTech in electronics and communication engineering from the Siliguri Institute of Technology. Besides academics, he is actively involved in the fields of robotics, IoT, and mobile application development. Since college, he has been involved with Microsoft as a Microsoft Student Partner and has organized 3-4 seminars and workshops on various Microsoft technologies, mainly on Windows Phone and Windows app development.

Being enthusiastic about robotics and Microsoft technologies, he has developed several robots, both autonomous and manual, and has developed a couple of manual robot controllers; some of these are the "Universal robot controller" for Windows PC and "Mark 1 Pilot" for Windows Phone. He is also into computer vision and has worked on detection of wild animals. A publication of his is *Automated Elephant Tracker* in the journal known as the *International journal of Electronics and Communication Engineering and Technology (IJECET)* under International Association for Engineering and Management Education, which includes his work on robotics and computer vision.

His website at http://www.avirupbasu.com holds some of his work, and you may get in touch with him there. Being a part-time blogger, he blogs about the topics he is interested in. Currently, he is working on autonomous robot control using SONAR and GPS. He dreams of carrying out research and development in his areas of interest.

Roberto Gallea, PhD, is a computer science researcher since 2007, at the University of Palermo, Italy. He is committed to investigating fields such as medical imaging, multimedia, and computer vision. In 2012, he started enhancing his academic and personal projects with the use of analog and digital electronics, with particular involvement in open source hardware and software platforms, such as Arduino. Besides his academic interests, he conducts personal projects aimed at producing hand-crafted items using embedded invisible electronics, such as musical instruments, furniture, and LED devices. Also, he collaborates with contemporary dance companies for digital scenes and costume designing.

Seyed Mohsen Mousavi received his telecommunication engineering bachelor's degree from Istanbul Technical University, and he is currently pursuing his master's in computer engineering at the same university. He works as an embedded software engineer in the research and development department of Turkcell Technology. He participated in the pioneering research and hands-on development of M2M and IoT in this company and has over 15 patents. His research interests focus on embedded systems, communication technologies, and computer vision. He has a passion for learning new technologies and making them work in real-life projects.

Surya Penmetsa is a 20-year-old recently graduated alumnus of NIT Warangal, specializing in electronics and communication engineering. Surya is mainly interested in the fields of image processing and computer vision, which form his core area of research. His other interests include making educational videos and broadcasting them on YouTube through the channel "The Motivated Engineer" which has been viewed more than 270,000 times at the time of writing this book. Apart from this, Surya enjoys exploring new fields and has completed more than 20 online courses learning new ideas.

I would like to offer my sincere gratitude especially to my parents, friends, and all the people associated at all stages of researching while reviewing the book for their support and unwavering motivation.

Randy Schur is a graduate student in mechanical engineering at The George Washington University. He has experience with Arduino, robotics, and rapid prototyping, and has worked on *Building Wireless Sensor Networks Using Arduino*, *Packt Publishing*.

www.PacktPub.com

Support files, eBooks, discount offers, and more

For support files and downloads related to your book, please visit www.PacktPub.com.

Did you know that Packt offers eBook versions of every book published, with PDF and ePub files available? You can upgrade to the eBook version at www.PacktPub.com and as a print book customer, you are entitled to a discount on the eBook copy. Get in touch with us at service@packtpub.com for more details.

At www.PacktPub.com, you can also read a collection of free technical articles, sign up for a range of free newsletters and receive exclusive discounts and offers on Packt books and eBooks.

https://www2.packtpub.com/books/subscription/packtlib

Do you need instant solutions to your IT questions? PacktLib is Packt's online digital book library. Here, you can search, access, and read Packt's entire library of books.

Why subscribe?

- Fully searchable across every book published by Packt
- Copy and paste, print, and bookmark content
- On demand and accessible via a web browser

Free access for Packt account holders

If you have an account with Packt at www.PacktPub.com, you can use this to access PacktLib today and view 9 entirely free books. Simply use your login credentials for immediate access.

This is dedicated to my family.

– Özen Özkaya

Table of Contents

Preface

Computer vision is the next level of sensing the environment, especially for modern machines. Many present-day devices try to mimic human capabilities with a limited set of resources. Moreover, most of these imitations can be seen as insufficient because generally they are too indirect to reflect real human capabilities, especially in terms of vision.

Even though the variations of the conventional sensors are huge; they are incapable of reflecting the power of human vision systems, which is one of the most complex perception capabilities of human beings. So, we surely need the visual information to make our electronic systems more intelligent. This is where computer vision starts.

A camera can be seen as the ultimate vision sensor, which is very close to the human vision sensing system. However, the problem is that using a camera as a vision sensor was simply too complex and very difficult in action. The purpose of this book is to make computer vision easy by dividing a complex problem into basic, realizable substeps. The best part is that we can make it easy for real-life applications!

When we deal with real-life applications, there is no doubt that there should be a way to interact with real life. Embedded systems are exactly standing for these physical interactions. Arduino is one of the most popular embedded system platforms that provides an easy way of prototyping with its huge community and learning sources. Along with its key properties, which will be discussed in detail later, Arduino is a perfect candidate for the physical life interaction of any vision system.

Arduino's role is clear in a vision system. In most cases, vision information is combined with the data from various kinds of traditional sensors, such as the temperature sensor, pressure sensor, and accelerometer. Additionally, we need a good tool to take physical actions after the vision process, for example, driving motors and opening lights. Hence, Arduino is very useful in collecting data from the environment and taking actions, especially because it has various libraries developed and shared by the communities, which make prototyping very fast.

Open Source Computer Vision (OpenCV) is a great open source library that contains lots of optimized algorithms. One of the most important advantages of OpenCV is that it is a multiplatform library that is able to work on Windows, Linux, Mac OS, and even Android and iOS! Another important point is that it is a matured library, which has the latest release 3.0 (and 2.4.11) at the moment (July 2015). Because of all these reasons, for all computer vision tasks in the book, we'll use OpenCV in action!

This book will combine the powers of Arduino and computer vision in a generalized, well-defined, and applicable way. The practices and approaches in the book can be used for any related problems and platforms. At the end of the book, the aim is to enable you to solve any type of real-life vision problem with all its components by using a generalized approach.

In each chapter, you will find examples of real-life practical application about the topics. To make it grounded, we will build a vision-enabled robot step by step in the chapter. You will observe that even though the contexts of the problems are very different, the approach to solve them is the same and easy!

What this book covers

Chapter 1, General Overview of Computer Vision Systems, explains the design blocks and architecture by introducing an efficient approach to the real-life vision problems.

Chapter 2, Fundamentals and Installation of OpenCV, tells us about the fundamentals of the OpenCV library and how to install and test it on different operating system platforms.

Chapter 3, Data Acquisition with OpenCV and Arduino, shows the efficient approach in collecting data from the environment with practical tips and real-world examples.

Chapter 4, Filtering Data with OpenCV, introduces the built-in filters of the library and how to select and implement those filters by considering the context of the application.

Chapter 5, Processing Vision Data with OpenCV, explores how to extract meaningful information from the vision data and how to make them ready for a recognition system.

Chapter 6, Recognition with OpenCV, talks about the methods to detect and recognize objects from a given scene by exploring artificial intelligence methods in a practical way.

Chapter 7, Communicating with Arduino Using OpenCV, reveals the communication capabilities of Arduino and comprehensive best practices to connect it with an OpenCV environment.

Chapter 8, Acting in the Real World with Arduino, demonstrates how to elegantly interact with real life via physical actions.

Chapter 9, Building a "Click-to-Go" Robot, will give an all-in-one practical robot design and development example by combining everything you've learned. This chapter will also handle the problem-independent success of the suggested approach.

What you need for this book

The purpose of this book is to teach you how to develop computer vision-enabled systems that can interact with real life. All the required software to go through is free. Optionally, you can use alternative nonfree software to develop your application in case of any need.

Computer vision applications are developed by using OpenCV. Eclipse, Xcode, and Visual Studio are presented as integrated development environments. The embedded system parts of the applications are developed by using Arduino Uno R3 and the Arduino IDE.

Some of the chapter applications require electronic components, such as sensors or communication modules. All these modules are inexpensive and easy to find. The ideas behind the applications are generic and applicable to all kinds of related fields.

Who this book is for

This book is intended primarily for anyone who wants to carry their projects to a vision-enabled field to create more intelligent systems. Especially consumers and hobbyists who wish to learn computer vision programming with Arduino.

Robotics is one of the most popular fields of hobby electronics. We can simply say that with the content of this book, it will be possible to build robots that can see and make reasoning. The same scheme is valid for all other fields of consumer and/or hobby electronics. Anyone who is excited about such schemes is part of the intended audience.

It is assumed that the reader is familiar with the basics of Arduino. No knowledge of computer vision programming is required to start.

Conventions

In this book, you will find a number of styles of text that distinguish between different kinds of information. Here are some examples of these styles, and an explanation of their meaning.

Code words in text, database table names, folder names, filenames, file extensions, pathnames, dummy URLs, user input, and Twitter handles are shown as follows: "We can include other contexts through the use of the `include` directive."

A block of code is set as follows:

```
#include <opencv2/highgui/highgui.hpp>
#include <iostream>

using namespace cv;
using namespace std;

int main( int argc, char** argv )
{
    Mat image_frame;
```

When we wish to draw your attention to a particular part of a code block, the relevant lines or items are set in bold:

```
#include <opencv2/highgui/highgui.hpp>
#include <iostream>

using namespace cv;
using namespace std;

int main( int argc, char** argv )
{
    Mat image_frame;
```

Any command-line input or output is written as follows:

```
sudo mkdir build
```

New terms and **important words** are shown in bold. Words that you see on the screen, in menus or dialog boxes for example, appear in the text like this: "Then, click on **Build Phases | Link Binary with Libraries** and click (**+**) to add the two required frameworks."

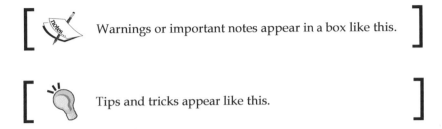

> Warnings or important notes appear in a box like this.

> Tips and tricks appear like this.

Reader feedback

Feedback from our readers is always welcome. Let us know what you think about this book—what you liked or may have disliked. Reader feedback is important for us to develop titles that you really get the most out of.

To send us general feedback, simply send an e-mail to feedback@packtpub.com, and mention the book title via the subject of your message.

If there is a topic that you have expertise in and you are interested in either writing or contributing to a book, see our author guide on www.packtpub.com/authors.

Customer support

Now that you are the proud owner of a Packt book, we have a number of things to help you to get the most from your purchase.

Downloading the example code

You can download the example code files for all Packt books you have purchased from your account at http://www.packtpub.com. If you purchased this book elsewhere, you can visit http://www.packtpub.com/support and register to have the files e-mailed directly to you.

Downloading the color images of this book

We also provide you with a PDF file that has color images of the screenshots/ diagrams used in this book. The color images will help you better understand the changes in the output. You can download this file from: `http://www.packtpub.com/sites/default/files/downloads/2627OS_ColorImages.pdf`.

Errata

Although we have taken every care to ensure the accuracy of our content, mistakes do happen. If you find a mistake in one of our books—maybe a mistake in the text or the code—we would be grateful if you could report this to us. By doing so, you can save other readers from frustration and help us improve subsequent versions of this book. If you find any errata, please report them by visiting `http://www.packtpub.com/submit-errata`, selecting your book, clicking on the **Errata Submission Form** link, and entering the details of your errata. Once your errata are verified, your submission will be accepted and the errata will be uploaded to our website or added to any list of existing errata under the Errata section of that title.

To view the previously submitted errata, go to `https://www.packtpub.com/books/content/support` and enter the name of the book in the search field. The required information will appear under the **Errata** section.

Piracy

Piracy of copyright material on the Internet is an ongoing problem across all media. At Packt, we take the protection of our copyright and licenses very seriously. If you come across any illegal copies of our works, in any form, on the Internet, please provide us with the location address or website name immediately so that we can pursue a remedy.

Please contact us at `copyright@packtpub.com` with a link to the suspected pirated material.

We appreciate your help in protecting our authors, and our ability to bring you valuable content.

Questions

You can contact us at `questions@packtpub.com` if you are having a problem with any aspect of the book, and we will do our best to address it.

1
General Overview of Computer Vision Systems

In this chapter, you will learn about the fundamentals and the general scheme of a computer vision system. The chapter will enable you to take a wide perspective when approaching computer vision problems.

Introducing computer vision systems

We use our five senses to observe everything around us—touch, taste, smell, hearing, and vision. Although all of these five senses are crucial, there is a sense which creates the biggest impact on perception. It is the main topic of this book and, undoubtedly, it is vision.

When looking at a scene, we understand and interpret the details within a meaningful context. This seems easy but it is a very complex process which is really hard to model. What makes vision easy for human eyes and hard for devices? The answer is hidden in the difference between human and machine perception. Many researchers are trying to go even further.

One of the most important milestones on the journey is the invention of the camera. Even though a camera is a good tool to save vision-based memories of scenes, it can lead to much more than just saving scenes. Just as with the invention of the camera, man has always tried to build devices to make life better. As the current trend is to develop intelligent devices, being aware of the environment around us is surely a crucial step in this. It is more or less the same for us; vision makes the biggest difference to the game. Thanks to technology, it is possible to mimic the human visual system and implement it on various types of devices. In the process we are able to build vision-enabled devices.

Images and timed series of images can be called video, in other words the computed representations of the real world. Any vision-enabled device recreates real scenes via images. Because extracting interpretations and hidden knowledge from images via devices is complex, computers are generally used for this purpose. The term, **computer vision**, comes from the modern approach of enabling machines to understand the real world in a human-like way. Since computer vision is necessary to automate daily tasks with devices or machines, it is growing quickly, and lots of frameworks, tools and libraries have already been developed.

Open Source Computer Vision Library (OpenCV) changed the game in computer vision and lots of people contributed to it to make it even better. Now it is a mature library which provides state-of-the-art design blocks which are handled in subsequent sections of this book. Because it is an easy-to-use library, you don't need to know the complex calculations under-the-hood to achieve vision tasks. This simplicity makes sophisticated tasks easy, but even so you should know how to approach problems and how to use design tools in harmony.

Approaching computer vision problems

To be able to solve any kind of complex problem such as a computer vision problem, it is crucial to divide it into simple and realizable substeps by understanding the purpose of each step. This chapter aims to show you how to approach any computer vision problem and how to model the problem by using a generic model template.

A practical computer vision architecture, explained in this book, consists of the combination of an Arduino system and an OpenCV system, as shown in the following diagram:

Arduino is solely responsible for collecting the sensory information—such as temperature, or humidity—from the environment and sending this information to the vision controller OpenCV system. The communication between the vision controller system and the Arduino system can be both wired or wireless as Arduino can handle both easily. After the vision system processes the data from Arduino and the webcam, it comes to a detection (or recognition) conclusion. For example, it can even recognize your face. The next step is acting on this conclusion by sending commands to the Arduino system and taking the appropriate actions. These actions might be driving a fan to make the environment cooler, moving a robotic arm to pass your coffee, and so on!

> A vision controller can be a desktop computer, laptop, mobile phone or even a microcomputer such as Raspberry Pi, or Beaglebone! OpenCV works on all of these platforms, so the principles are valid for all of these platforms. Microcomputers are also able to do some of the work otherwise done by Arduino.

Any computer vision system consists of well-defined design blocks ordered by data acquisition, preprocessing, image processing, post filtering, recognition (or detection) and actuation. This book will handle all of these steps in detail with a practical approach. We can draw a generic diagram of a computer vision system by mapping the steps to the related implementation platforms. In the following diagram, you can find a generic process view of a computer vision system:

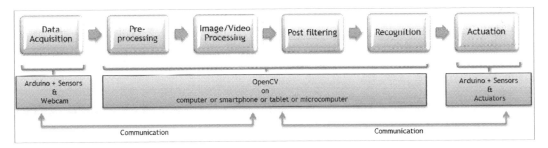

Data acquisition

As can be seen, the first step is data acquisition, which normally collects the sensory information from the environment. Within the perspective of the vision controller, there are two main data sources—the camera, and the Arduino system.

The camera is the ultimate sensor to mimic the human vision system and it is directly connected to the vision controller in our scheme. By using OpenCV's data acquisition capabilities, the vision controller reads the vision data from the camera. This data is either an image snapshot or a video created from the timed series of image frames. The camera can be of various types and categories.

In the most basic categorization, a camera can give out analog or digital data. All of the cameras used in the examples in this book are digital because the processing environment and processing operation itself are also digital. Each element of the picture is referred to as a pixel. In digital imaging, a pixel, pel, or picture element is a physical point in a raster image or the smallest addressable element in an all-points-addressable display device; so it is the smallest controllable element of a picture represented on the screen. You can find more information on this at http://en.wikipedia.org/wiki/Pixel.

Cameras can also be classified by their color sensing capabilities. RGB cameras are able to sense both main color components and a huge amount of combinations of these colors. Grayscale cameras are able to detect the scene only in terms of shades of gray. Hence, rather than color information, these cameras provide shape information. Lastly, binary cameras sense the scene only in black or white. By the way, a pixel in a binary camera can have only two values—black and white.

Another classification for cameras is their communication interface. Some examples are a USB camera, IP camera, wireless camera, and so on. The communication interface of the camera also directly affects the usability and capability of that camera. At home generally we have web cameras with USB interfaces. When using USB web cameras, generally you don't need external power sources or the external stuff that makes using the camera harder, so it is really easy to use a USB webcam for image processing tasks. Cameras also have properties such as resolution but we'll handle camera properties in forthcoming chapters.

Regular USB cameras, most often deployed as webcams, offer a 2D image. In addition to 2D camera systems, we now have 3D camera systems which can detect the depth of each element in the scene. The best known example of 3D camera systems is probably Kinect, which is shown here:

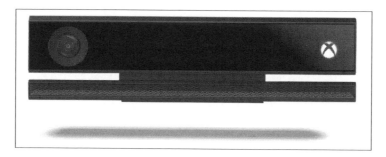

OpenCV supports various types of cameras, and it is possible to read the vision information from all these cameras by using simple interfaces, as this issue is handled by examples in the forthcoming chapters. Please keep in mind that image acquisition is the fundamental step of the vision process and we have lots of options.

Generally, we need information in addition to that from the camera to analyze the environment around us. Some of this information is related to our other four senses. Moreover, sometimes we need additional information beyond human capabilities. We can capture this information by using the Arduino sensors.

Imagine that you want to build a face-recognizing automatic door lock project. The system will probably be triggered by a door knock or a bell. You need a sound sensor to react when the door is knocked or the bell is rung. All of this information can be easily collected by Arduino. Let's add a fingerprint sensor to make it doubly safe! In this way, you can combine the data from the Arduino and the camera to reach a conclusion about the scene by running the vision system.

In conclusion, both the camera and the Arduino system (with sensors) can be used by the vision controller to capture the environment in detail!

Preprocessing

Preprocessing means getting something ready for processing. It can include various types of substeps but the principle is always the same. We will now explain preprocessing and why it is important in a vision system.

Firstly, let's make something clear. This step aims to make the collected vision data ready for processing. Preprocessing is required in computer vision systems since raw data is generally noisy. In the image data we get from the camera, we have lots of unneeded regions and sometimes we have a blurry image because of vibration, movement, and so on. In any case, it is better to filter the image to make it more useful for our system. For example, if you want to detect a big red ball in the image, you can just remove small dots, or you can even remove those parts which are not red. All of these kinds of filtering operations will make our life easy.

Generally, filtering is also done in data acquisition by the cameras, but every camera has different preprocessing capabilities and some of them even have vibration isolation. But, when built-in capabilities increase, cost is increased in parallel. So we'll handle how to do the filtering inside of our design via OpenCV. By the way, it is possible to design robust vision systems even with cheap equipment such as a webcam.

The same is valid for the sensor data. We always get noisy data in real life cases so noise should be filtered to get the actual information from the sensor. Some of these noises come from the environment and some of them come from the internal structure of the sensor. In any case, data should be made ready for processing; this book will give practical ways to achieve that end.

It should be understood that the complexity of image data is generally much greater than with any regular sensor such as a temperature sensor or a humidity sensor. The dimensions of the data which represents the information are also different. RGB images include three color components per pixel; red, green and blue. To represent a scene with a resolution of 640x480, a RGB camera needs 640x480x3 = 921600 bytes. Multiplication by three comes from the dimension of each pixel. Each pixel holds 3 bytes of data in total, 1 byte for each color. To represent the temperature of a room, we generally need 4 bytes of data. This also explains why we need highly capable devices to work on images. Moreover, the complexity of image filters is different from simple sensor filters.

But it doesn't mean that we cannot use complex filters in a simple way. If we know the purpose of the filter and the meanings of filter parameters, we can use them easily. This book aims to make you aware of the filtering process and how to apply advanced filtering techniques in an easy way.

So, filtering is for extracting the real information from the data and it is an integral step in the computer vision process. Many computer vision projects fail in the development phase because of the missing layer of filtering. Even the best recognition algorithms fail with noisy and inaccurate data. So, please be aware of the importance of data filtering and preprocessing.

Feature extraction by image processing

The most inspiring part of a computer vision project is probably the automated interpretation of the scene. To extract meanings from an image, we apply various types of image processing techniques. Sometimes we need more information than we can take from a single image. In this case, relationships between image frames become important. If such inter-frame information is extracted, it is called video processing. Some video processing applications also include the processing of audio signals. Because all the principles are same, video processing is not so much different from image processing.

To understand the importance of this chapter it is logical to look at real life applications. Imagine that you want to build a vision-enabled line-follower robot. There will be a camera on top of the middle of the robot and the robot will follow a black line on a white floor. To achieve this task you should detect the line and find out if the line is on the left side or the right side. If the line is on the left side of the image, you should go left to take it in to the middle. Similarly, if the line is on the right side of the image, you should go right. Within a margin, if a line is in the middle of the image, you should go forward. You can also detect the orientation of the line to plan your robot's movements in a smarter way.

In this example, you should apply image processing techniques to detect the line in the image. You will see that the book proposes a good, small set of techniques which show you the directions that you should follow to solve your problem. And, by applying these techniques, it is possible to get some candidate regions in the images which can be counted as a line. To interpret the line candidates efficiently, you should make feature extraction for the regions in the image. By comparing the features (properties) of the line candidates system you can separate real lines from noises, such as shadows.

Feature extraction is a pattern recognition and classification term that means extracting a small set of information which represents a bigger set of information. By processing images, we extract the so-called features such as length, position, area of an image region, and so on. Later on, we will use these features to detect and recognise any kinds of objects.

There are some major approaches to extract useful small sets of information from the image. Segmentation is a term for such an operation.

Image segmentation is the process of partitioning a digital image into multiple segments (sets of pixels, also known as superpixels). The goal of segmentation is to simplify and/or change the representation of an image into something that is more meaningful and easier to analyze.

More information can be found at
http://en.wikipedia.org/wiki/Image_segmentation.

In our example, line candidates are segments in the image.

Blob analysis is a good method that labels the segments in the image. It is a useful method to find the closed loops in the image. Closed loops generally correspond to objects in the image. Blob analysis is also an image processing technique and will be handled later. It is important to get the idea of the feature extraction now.

The information which was extracted from the image will be used in the next step of the computer vision system. Because this processing step will summarize the image, it is very important to do this correctly to make the whole vision system work. Again, you don't need to know the complex calculations under the hood. Instead, you should know where and how to use image processing techniques to get valuable small information sets from the scene. That is exactly what this book deals with in the forthcoming chapters.

Post-processing and post-filtering

After extracting some useful information from the image, sometimes a higher layer of filtering is required. The removal of unnecessary segments by considering their properties is one such higher level of filtering. Normally, it is very easy if you know the requirements of the related project.

Because this step is very simple, sometimes we can think of it as part of image processing. It also makes senses because the aim of image processing is to provide a small set of clear information to the recognition or detection element.

OpenCV has good mechanisms for post-processing and we'll handle them in a brief, practical way by basing the concepts on real life examples. Understanding the purpose itself is much more important.

Recognition or detection

The main purpose of the vision system is to reach a conclusion by interpreting the scheme via images or the image arrays. The way to the conclusion is recognition or detection.

Detection can be counted as a basic form of recognition. The aim is to detect an object or event. There are two types of conclusion. An object or an event either exists or it doesn't. Because of this binary nature of conclusion it is a special classification process with two classes. The first class is existence and the second class is non-existence. "To be or not to be, that is the question."

Recognition is a more complex term which is also called classification and tells the identification process of one or more pre-specified or learned objects or object classes. Face recognition is a good example of such an operation. A vision system should identify you by recognizing your face. This is generally a complex classification process with multiple classes. In this case, each face is a class, so it is a complex problem. But, thanks to OpenCV, we have lots of easy-to-use mechanisms for recognition, even for complex problems.

Sometimes, complex algorithms take a lot of time to finish. Similarly, in some cases, very fast behavior is needed, especially for real-time performance requirements. In such cases, we can also use simple but effective decision algorithms. As *Leonardo da Vinci* says, *"Simplicity is the ultimate sophistication"*. This book also will tell you about how to build robust recognition systems by using simple design blocks.

Again, you should be aware of the aim of recognition or classification. This awareness will show you the path which you should follow to succeed.

Acting in the real world

Every vision system has a purpose. There are some scenarios such as; "if you detect this event (or object), do this action". At the end of the long but enjoyable decision process of a vision system, the next step would surely be to perform an action by considering the conclusion. This is because of the "existence purpose" of the system. Everything up to now has been done to enable us to take the right action.

Let's remember our line follower robot example. The robot detects the line and the position of the line in its view. It also decides on the direction to follow. Would it be meaningful if the robot knew the direction in which it should go but was unable to move? This example also shows the importance of the action at the end.

The physical action managed by the vision controller should affect real life in a physical manner. Good examples are driving motors to move on, heating an environment, unlocking a door, triggering a device, and so on. To do this leads us to the Arduino. It has a huge amount of community support, lots of libraries on many devices and it is really easy to use. Maybe for industrial design, you can go beyond Arduino but it is a fact that Arduino is a very good proof-of-concept platform for physical interaction with the world. Arduino is an embedded system which makes the hard engineering stuff simple and easy. So we should love it!

The most inspiring thing about using embedded systems to produce different physical interactions is that many of them are the same in terms of software development. Square wave signals are used for different purposes in embedded systems. You will learn about them in detail in later chapters but consider that square waves can be used for a kind of dimming functionality. When you produce a square wave with fifty percent duty ratio; it means that there will be a pulse with logic high in a limited time t and with a logic low in a limited time t. The software will apply the same dimming principle even on completely different devices. If you apply this fairly high frequency square wave to a motor, it will turn at half of its speed capability. Similarly, if you apply the same square wave to an LED, it will shine at half of its shining capability. Even with completely different physical devices, we have the same behavior with the same software. So, we should see the inspiring nature of the instruments which we use to touch the world and if we have an idea of how to connect them to our system then everything will be okay.

In this book we present a hardware-independent software approach to interact with the world. So, even though the physical examples are hardware-dependent, you will be able to apply the same principles to any embedded system. There are also state-of-the art tips to interact with the world using Arduino in an artistic way.

Connecting the pieces

In the approach we have presented, the vision process is divided into well-defined, easy-to-realize sub-blocks. Because every block has a major role in the performance of the overall system, each of them should be developed efficiently under some simple principles which will make the vision system rock solid.

When approaching any kind of vision problem, firstly the big picture should be seen and the problem should be divided into meaningful and internally independent sub-pieces as we proposed. This approach will make you see important details and isolated solutions to small problems. This is the most important first step to building futuristic vision-enabled systems. The next step is just connecting the pieces and enjoying your art!

The approach which is presented in this chapter is applicable to any kind of vision system. But you should get more and more practice in real life situations to ground the approach solidly. Let's do some brainstorming on such a real-life example—a hand gesture-controlled door unlock system.

There should be a camera at the entrance, by the door, which is able to see any guest's movements. To make it more applicable let's trigger the motion detection system by pressing the bell. Visitors will press the bell and show a right hand gesture to the camera, and the vision controller will unlock the door automatically. If the hand gesture is wrong, the door won't open.

The first step is data acquisition and, because we want to see hand gestures, we can use a simple 30FPS webcam with a 1024x768 resolution.

We can convert the image to binary and we can apply a filter to remove small objects in the image. The hand will be presented in a binary way. Filtering is done.

Now we should perform feature extraction to find the possible position of the hand in the image. The convex hull method or blob analysis can be used for such a problem and we will handle these algorithms later on. At the end, we will have an image with features of hand candidates, as shown in this screenshot:

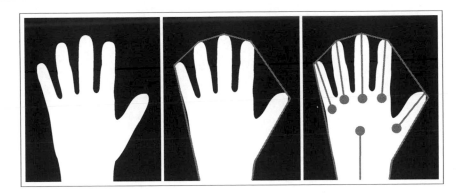

We need a hand detector as the next step. We can use the number of fingers by applying a skeleton analysis to the hand and by comparing the positions of the fingers; we can classify the hand gesture.

If it is the right hand gesture, we can send the information to the Arduino door unlock controller and it will unlock the door for a limited time to welcome the authorized visitor!

You can apply all these principals to any problem to get familiar with it. Do not focus on the algorithmic details now. Just try to divide the problem into pieces and try to decide what properties you can use to solve the problem.

As long as you get used to the approach, this book will show you how to realize each step and how you can find the right algorithm to achieve it. So, go on and try to repeat the approach for a garage door open/close system which will recognize your car's number plate!

Summary

We now know how to approach vision projects and how to divide them into isolated pieces which make the realization of the projects much easier. We also have some idea about how the complex tasks of vision systems can be achieved in a systematic way.

We also talked about the reason and importance of each sub-step in the approach. We are now aware of the key points in the approach and have a solid knowledge of how we can define a solution frame for any computer vision problem.

Now, it is time to get your hands dirty!

2

Fundamentals and Installation of OpenCV

Open Source Computer Vision (OpenCV), is a computer vision library that is used by academics, commercial companies, embedded electronic enthusiast communities and hobbyists all around the world. OpenCV has C++, C, Python, and Java interfaces and supports Windows, Linux, Mac OS, Android, and iOS. It is designed for computational efficiency and ease of use with a focus on real-time applications. Algorithms are optimized and suitable to run on different hardware platforms, even on multiple cores! Indeed, one advantage is that OpenCV has a user community base of around 50,000 people. Its range of use is broad, from object recognition to motion detection, and probably the best part is that it is really popular among the robotics community. Let's dive in to this computer vision realm by introducing OpenCV modules.

Fundamentals of OpenCV

In this section, we'll talk about OpenCV components to give you a better understanding of the structure and provide some information about the fundamentals of OpenCV. You will get insight into the modules so you will able to add whatever is needed in your upcoming Arduino/OpenCV chapter projects. So, get ready to learn about the modules! The modules we are talking about include both shared and static libraries. There are many capabilities OpenCV has to offer to give an easy-to-use experience to users. Because of that we are able to truly focus on projects. For the latest stable version, the following modules are available:

- **opencv_core**: This neat module defines basic data structures that we will use constantly, including the dense multi-dimensional array Mat and the basic functions used by all other modules.

- **opencv_imgproc**: With the help of the image processing module, we can tinker with the raw images like a professional to prepare them for the further steps of computer vision. In this module, we have linear and non-linear image filtering, geometrical image transformations, color space conversion, histograms, and many more.

- **opencv_video**: Now things are getting real-time with the help of the video module. We can assess very important inter-frame capabilities such as motion estimation, background subtraction, and object tracking algorithms.

- **opencv_calib3d**: This multiple-view module gives the ability to manipulate multiple camera frames for adding a new dimension to our work space. This controls depth information extraction.

- **opencv_feature2d**: This module makes it possible to use edge and corner detections with plenty of fast and real-time algorithms. We will see how important it is to have feature detectors, descriptors and descriptor matchers in our projects.

- **opencv_objdetect**: After extracting some main features with the preceding modules, we can now detect objects and instances of the predefined classes (for example, faces, eyes, mugs, people, cars, and so on).

- **opencv_highgui**: This module is an interface with awesome UI capabilities. We will use GUI features to better understand the captured and processed data.

- **opencv_videoio**: This module is an interface to video capturing and video codecs. We will use this module very frequently for real-time data acquisition in applications.

- **opencv_gpu**: GPU-accelerated algorithms from different OpenCV modules.

There are other helper modules, such as FLANN and Google test wrappers, Python bindings, and so on.

Get ready to discover these modules in the next few chapters. But first, make sure to get OpenCV ready on the platform you are using for the development! The next section will guide you through the installation of the library. We will get our hands dirty!

The installation of OpenCV

This section will cover the installation procedure for OpenCV in Windows, Linux, Mac OS, iOS, and Android. Newer versions of the OpenCV library are released periodically. As it is the latest stable version, the 2.4.10 version of OpenCV is used in this book. It is worth noting that the installation principles for future releases will be more or less the same because of OpenCV's maturity and stability.

Installing OpenCV on Linux

We would like to start with the Linux installation process. The reason is that Linux runs not only on laptops and workstations but is also very popular on embedded Linux platforms such as Raspberry Pi, and BeagleBone Black. You can simply install and run OpenCV projects by following the steps that we are about to track. We have used Ubuntu 12.04 LTS for this installation. Before you install OpenCV, especially for embedded Linux platforms, you will need to check that you have all of the required elements, listed as follows:

- **Disk space**: 2 GB is the minimum recommended. You will require more free space to store your teaching materials.
- **Memory**: 256 MB (minimum); 1 GB (recommended).

Installing and configuring packages

We are about to install OpenCV 2.4.10 from its website. You can download this version from http://opencv.org/downloads.html. Now let's follow these steps for preparing your development environment:

1. Go to http://opencv.org/downloads.html, scroll down, and click **OpenCV for Linux/Mac** under **VERSION 2.4.10**.

2. Unzip the package to your desktop; any place other than the desktop is okay as long as you know the location of the package.

3. Open the terminal by pressing *Ctrl + Alt + T* and enter these commands for installing dependencies of OpenCV:

```
sudo apt-get install build-essential libgtk2.0-dev libjpeg-dev
libtiff4-dev libjasper-dev libopenexr-dev cmake python-dev
python-numpy python-tk libtbb-dev libeigen3-dev yasm libfaac-
dev libopencore-amrnb-dev libopencore-amrwb-dev libtheora-dev
libvorbis-dev libxvidcore-dev libx264-dev libqt4-dev libqt4-
opengl-dev sphinx-common texlive-latex-extra libv4l-dev
libdc1394-22-dev libavcodec-dev libavformat-dev libswscale-dev
default-jdk ant libvtk5-qt4-dev
```

4. Open the terminal by pressing *Ctrl + Alt +T* and navigate to the package for installation by entering this command:

```
cd Desktop/opencv-2.4.10
```

5. Create a `build` folder and go into it to create the make file:

```
sudo mkdir build
cd build
sudo cmake ..
```

6. Run this command to start the installation of the version:

```
sudo make
sudo make install
```

You should now see the installation process on the terminal window.

7. You have to configure OpenCV. First, open the `opencv.conf` file with the following code:

```
sudo gedit /etc/ld.so.conf/opencv.conf
```

8. Add the following line at the end of the file (it may be an empty file, which is fine) and then save it:

```
/usr/local/lib
```

9. Run the following code to configure the library:

```
sudo ldconfig
```

10. Now you have to open another file:

```
sudo gedit /etc/bash.bashrc
```

11. Add the corresponding lines at the end of the file to make the OpenCV locations visible to the whole operating system and save it:

```
PKG_CONFIG_PATH=$PKG_CONFIG_PATH:/usr/local/lib/pkgconfig
export PKG_CONFIG_PATH
```

12. Finally, restart the computer. OpenCV may not work correctly unless you follow this restart procedure.

Using OpenCV with Eclipse CDT

Eclipse is a cross-platform **Integrated Development Environment (IDE)**. It is convenient and efficient to develop code on an IDE instead of with a simple editor. We will use Eclipse because it is free, suitable for object oriented coding, and popular among coders. Another benefit of using Eclipse is that when we have an error, we will be warned! This feature is very useful when working with a new library. In this book we'll give examples in C/C++. For this reason, Eclipse CDT is the recommended development environment.

Installing Eclipse CDT

Let's install Eclipse on your workstation (only the CDT plugin for C/C++ is needed). You can perform the following steps:

1. Download Eclipse IDE for C/C++ Developers. Choose the link according to your workstation.

2. Launch the executable file.

3. Follow the on-screen instructions to install Eclipse.

To make a project, follow these steps:

1. Start Eclipse and run the executable that comes in the folder.

2. Go to **File | New | C/C++ Project | C++ Project**. Click **Next**.

3. Choose a name for your project (for example, OpenCV_Template).
   An **Empty Project** should be selected for this project example.
   In addition, select **Linux GCC**.

4. Leave everything else as the default. Press **Finish**.

5. The project should appear in the **Project Navigator** (on the left side
   of the window).

6. Add a source file for the OpenCV code.

7. Right-click the OpenCV_Template project, then select **New | Folder**.

8. Name the folder src by convention and click **Finish**.

9. Right-click on the newly created folder src. Choose **New source file**. Name it
   main.cpp and then click **Finish**.

10. Now you have a project with an empty .cpp file. Let's copy and paste the test
    code given here:

```cpp
#include "opencv2/opencv.hpp"
using namespace cv;
int main(int, char**)
{
    VideoCapture cap(0);
    if(!cap.isOpened())
        return -1;
namedWindow("frame", CV_WINDOW_AUTOSIZE);
    for(;;)
    {
        Mat frameIn;
        cap >> frameIn;
imshow("frame", frameIn);
        if(waitKey(30) >= 0) break;
    }
return 0;
}
```

Downloading the example code

You can download the example code files from your account at
`http://www.packtpub.com` for all the Packt Publishing books
you have purchased. If you purchased this book elsewhere, you can
visit `http://www.packtpub.com/support` and register to have
the files e-mailed directly to you.

Let's explain the source code briefly before going any further. These are the first two
lines of code:

```
#include "opencv2/opencv.hpp"
using namespace cv;
```

The first line shows the compiler where to find the necessary functions related to
OpenCV. The file `opencv.hpp` shows the addresses of OpenCV modules.

The second line gives information to the editor about the namespace the code
is using.

The following is the main code body:

```
VideoCapture cap(0);
if(!cap.isOpened())
        return -1;
namedWindow("frame", CV_WINDOW_AUTOSIZE);
```

In the first line the `VideoCapture` object is created to capture a video stream from
one of the built-in webcams or externally connected webcams.

The `if(!cap.isOpened())` statement checks whether the object created has been
successfully opened or not.

A window to show the captured webcam stream is created with the name of the frame
with the `namedWindow` function and the `CV_WINDOW_AUTOSIZE` sizing parameter.

Then, if everything goes well, the code starts to display captured webcam frames.
This is the `for` loop body:

```
for(;;)
{
        Mat frameIn;
        cap >> frameIn;
        imshow("frame", frameIn);
        if(waitKey(30) >= 0) break;
}
```

The code starts to run in the for(;;) loop to show the captured image if no key is pressed. The captured image is loaded to frameIn and it is shown in the frame namedWindow by calling the imshow function.

We have one more step to go. It is to tell OpenCV where the OpenCV headers and libraries are. To achieve this, do the following:

1. Go to **Project | Properties**, and then follow these steps:

    1. In **C/C++ Build**, click on the **Settings | Tool Settings** tab. Here we will enter the headers and libraries info.

    2. In GCC C++ Compiler, go to Includes. In **Include paths**(-1) you should include the path of the folder where OpenCV was installed. In our example, this is /usr/local/include/opencv.

    3. Now go to **GCC C++ Linker** where you have to fill two spaces:

        First, in **Library search path** (-L), you have to write the path to where the OpenCV libraries reside:

        `/usr/local/lib`

        Then, in **Libraries(-l)**, add the OpenCV libraries that we may need:

        ```
        opencv_core opencv_imgproc opencv_highgui opencv_ml opencv_
        video opencv_features2d opencv_calib3d opencv_objdetect
        opencv_contrib opencv_legacy opencv_flan
        ```

        If you don't know where your libraries are, type in the terminal:

        `pkg-config --libs opencv`

        to check the location of your OpenCV library.

        The output should look something like the following:

        ```
        -L/usr/local/lib -lopencv_core -lopencv_imgproc -lopencv
        highgui -lopencv_ml  lopencv_video -lopencv_features2d
        -lopencv_calib3d -lopencv_objdetect -lopencv_contrib
        -lopencv_legacy -lopencv_flann
        ```

2. Now you are done. Click **OK**

Your project should be ready to be built. For this, go to **Project | Build all** in the console. Now you are ready to go!

Installing OpenCV on Mac OS

If you are reading this part you are a Mac developer! Apple has established a very rich development environment. Xcode is free and very smooth on Mac OS, as would be expected. Let's get Xcode then! You can get Xcode from Mac App Store or at `https://developer.apple.com/xcode/downloads/`.

Getting command-line tools

Press the `spacebar` and `cmd` keys at the same time in order to open the **Spotlight Search** window. Then, type terminal and open it. Type the following commands into it:

```
xcode-select --install
```

Installing HomeBrew

HomeBrew helps us to install OpenCV. To download Homebrew, run the following install script on the command line and let the script do its thing:

```
ruby -e "$(curl -fsSL
https://raw.githubusercontent.com/Homebrew/install/master/install)"
```

Also update and upgrade right away by running the following commands. This step will ensure everything about HomeBrew is up to date:

```
brew update
```

```
brew upgrade
```

Once you have HomeBrew installed you can go ahead and add `homebrew/science` where OpenCV is located, using:

```
brew tap homebrew/science
```

Let's enter this command to start the installation:

```
brew install opencv
```

You're done! You can find OpenCV at the following location. Type this command:

```
cd /usr/local/Cellar/opencv/2.4.10.1/
```

In order to make sure OpenCV is linked to Xcode, type this command:

```
brew link opencv
```

After confirming it, we can now link the required libraries to Xcode.

Using OpenCV in Xcode

To use the OpenCV libraries you need to create a C++ project and tell Xcode where to find the OpenCV libraries.

1. Create a command-line tool by selecting **Xcode | File | Project... | OS X | Application | Command Line Tool** and click **Next**.

2. After that, name your project OpenCV_Template. Select **Language** as **C++** and click **Next**.

3. Select where to store your project and click **Finish**.

4. Click the Xcode project file from the window. You need to have three tabs at the top of the page: **Build Settings**, **Build Phases**, and **Build Rules**.

5. Click **Build Settings** and look for **Search Paths**. Double-click the **Header Search Paths** option, then click the plus (**+**) icon to add a new path. The path is /usr/local/include.

6. Next double-click the **Library Search Paths** option, then click the (**+**) plus icon. Add /usr/local/lib.

As a final step, we need to add the Xcode OpenCV Binaries by following these steps:

1. OpenCV binaries need to be added to the project. For this purpose, you need to go to **Build Phases**.

2. Click **Link Binary With Libraries | Add Other...**.

3. Click the plus (**+**) icon to add libraries. To do this, click **Shift**, **cmd** and the **g** buttons and go to /usr/local/lib.

4. Select libopencv_*.dylib and add to the project.

Now it is time to test our first OpenCV project with Xcode!

You are ready to run your test code. Copy and paste the test code, given in the *Using OpenCV with Eclipse CDT* section, into the main.cpp file.

Installing OpenCV on Windows

Windows is a common operating system and lots of OpenCV users use it. In this section, we will explain the installation procedure for OpenCV with Windows. This procedure should work on all Windows versions since linking OpenCV for every version of Windows is very similar. Our current configuration is Windows 8, 64-bit OS, OpenCV 2.4.10. Put simply, we are introducing OpenCV to Windows to let it know where to look when OpenCV is needed.

Install pre-built libraries by following these steps:

1. Launch `opencv.org` from your browser and click the link, **OpenCV for Windows**.

2. Run the corresponding `opencv-2.4.10.exe` which is downloaded after clicking the `OpenCV for Windows.exe` file.

3. Extract the files to `C:/`.

You need to add the necessary paths to link the libraries to the project you are about to create.

1. Open **Control Panel | System | Advanced system settings | Advanced | Environment variables | System variables**.

2. In **System variables**, scroll down until you find **Path**, select it and click **Edit**.

3. On the **Edit System Variable** window add `;C:\opencv\build\x64\vc12\bin;` at the very end of the variable value. Finally, click **OK**.

 Note: Please be careful *NOT to delete* variable values while adding; `C:\opencv\build\x64\vc12\bin;`

A semicolon is used to separate variable values. Make sure you use them!

It is better to restart your computer to make sure the system recognizes the environment path variables. If everything goes well you are good to go for the next step that is creating a new OpenCV project.

Installing MS Visual Studio 2013

Get MS Visual Studio 2013 by visiting `https://www.visualstudio.com/en-us/downloads/download-visual-studio-vs.aspx`. Install MS Visual Studio 2013.

1. After installing MS Visual Studio, select **File | New | Project... | Visual C++ Win32 | Win32 Console Application**. Give a name to your project. Let's set the name as `OpenCV_Template`. Set the project location. For instance, `C:\OpenCV_Projects`. Lastly, click **OK**.

2. **The Win32 Application Wizard** window will appear, click **Next |** and put a check mark against **Additional options:(Empty Project)** and click **Finish**.

3. Right-click on the project, `OpenCV_Template`, and click **Properties**.

4. Add given paths to **C/C++ | General | Additional Include Directories | Click on <Edit...>**:

```
C:\opencv\build\include
C:\opencv\build\include\opencv
C:\opencv\build\include\opencv2
```

5. Add a given path to **Linker | General | Additional Include Directories | Click on <Edit...>**:

```
C:\opencv\build\x64\vc12\lib
```

6. Go to and add given opencv_xd.libs to **Linker | Input | Additional Dependencies | Click on <Edit...>**:

```
opencv_calib3d2410d.lib
opencv_contrib2410d.lib
opencv_core2410d.lib
opencv_features2d2410d.lib
opencv_flann2410d.lib
opencv_gpu2410d.lib
opencv_highgui2410d.lib
opencv_imgproc2410d.lib
opencv_legacy2410d.lib
opencv_ml2410d.lib
opencv_nonfree2410d.lib
opencv_objdetect2410d.lib
opencv_ocl2410d.lib
opencv_photo2410d.lib
opencv_stitching2410d.lib
opencv_superres2410d.lib
opencv_ts2410d.lib
opencv_video2410d.lib
opencv_videostab2410d.lib
```

Filenames prefixed with d denote debug purpose libraries. Another important thing to know is that version numbers of the .libs need to be the same as for the version you installed. Lets say you installed OpenCV 2.4.9, the filenames should resemble opencv_core249d.lib.

Now you are ready to go one step forward.

7. Go to **OpenCV_Template** and right-click **Source Files | New Item... | Visual C++ | C++ File**, naming the source file as `main.cpp`.

8. Finally, copy and paste the given code in the *Using OpenCV with Eclipse CDT* section.

OpenCV on iOS

Devices such as iPhones and iPads are very popular in the developer community. Offering an application that is capable of processing an image is a fancy way of showing off your abilities to your hobbyist friends. Imagine that you have an iPhone controlling your line-following robot. Your iPhone is sending commands to your robot via Bluetooth to follow the line! We are almost ready to start development focused on iOS. In order to run your application on a real device you have to be a registered Apple developer and pay the subscription fee ($99 per year) for the iOS Developer Program. If you don't want to pay this fee you can always use a simulator as the device.

Now you are about to launch your first OpenCV iOS project. Lets ensure that you installed Xcode. You can check the **Install OpenCV on Mac OS** section.

1. Create a new Xcode project for iOS, Let's name it `OpenCV_iOS_Template`.

2. Download `opencv2.framework` from `http://sourceforge.net/projects/opencvlibrary/files/opencv-ios/3.0.0-beta/opencv2.framework.zip/download` and unpack it.

3. You need to link `opencv2.framework` with Xcode. Select the project Navigator in the left side of the window and click on the project name.

4. Click **Build Phases | Link Binary With Libraries** then click plus (+) to add the `opencv2.framework`. Alternatively, you can drag and drop the `opencv2.framework`.

5. Lastly, right-click your project and **New File... | PCH File** and add this code to the newly created `OpenCV_iOS_Template.pch`.

   ```
   ifdef __cplusplus
   #import <opencv2/opencv.hpp>
   #endif
   ```

Now you are ready to focus on your iOS project!

OpenCV on Android

Imagine that you can turn your Android phone into a real-time image processing platform which could be implemented to your robotics project. Android is a powerful platform with a wide range of capabilities which can boost your vision applications. So let's open the door to making our vision-enabled applications mobile! You can put your Android phone on top of your robot and use it as the eye of the robot! We will set up the environment needed for this purpose in this section. To create OpenCV Android applications you need to install the denominated prerequisites. For this process we will follow several steps.

Installing OpenCV4Android

You can download the OpenCV4Android package from: `http://sourceforge.net/projects/opencvlibrary/files/opencv-android/`. The latest version is `OpenCV-2.4.11-android-sdk.zip`.

As with the next step for Windows, extract the SDK to the `C:\opencv4android` directory. You can use any kind of archiver, such as `Winrar`. On Linux, you can use the following command to extract the archive:

```
unzip ~/Downloads/OpenCV-2.4.11-android-sdk.zip
```

The current development environment for Android is Android Studio. But OpenCV4Android SDK does not directly support Android Studio. It is easy to use it with Eclipse with the **Android Developer Tools (ADT)** bundle. So Eclipse is preferred in this book.

 It is possible to develop OpenCV applications for Android by using the C++ API. To do this, you should also install the Android Native Development Kit (NDK) from `https://developer.android.com/tools/sdk/ndk/index.html`.

Eclipse integration

By installing the Eclipse ADT bundle, you get an Android-ready version of Eclipse! You can download it from:

```
https://dl.google.com/android/adt/adt-bundle-windows-x86_64-20140702.zip
```

This tutorial is summarized at: `http://docs.opencv.org/doc/tutorials/introduction/android_binary_package/O4A_SDK.html`.

Follow the given steps:

1. Start Eclipse and choose your workspace location as the `C:\opencv4android` directory.

2. The `Opencv4Android` library is ready to use projects. Import the OpenCV library and samples into the workspace. Right-click on the **Package Explorer** window and choose the **Import...** option from the context menu, as shown in this screenshot:

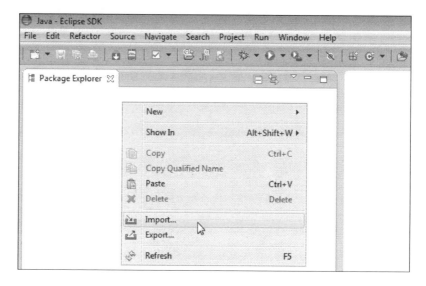

3. In the main panel, select **General | Existing Projects into Workspace** and press the **Next** button.

4. Select the **C:\opencv4android** directory as the root directory and all the projects will be listed. Then click **Finish**.

 After the initial import, on a non-Windows operating system (Linux and Mac OS), Eclipse will still show build errors for applications with native C++ code. To resolve these issues, please do the following:

Open **Project Properties | C/C++ Build**, and replace the **Build command** text with `${NDKROOT}/ndk-build` (remove `.cmd` at the end).

5. Once Eclipse completes the build you will have a clean workspace without any build errors, as shown here:

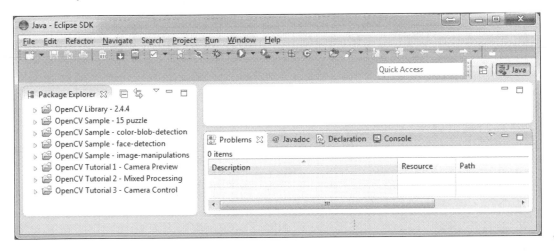

Running samples

Before running samples, go to Google Play and install OpenCV Manager and the OCV 2.4 pack armeabi-v7a applications from Google Play. The binary application OCV 2.4 pack armeabi-v7a is a hardware-specific application but it will work with most Android devices. For older devices you can install the appropriate APK file by using the following tip:

To find the appropriate version of the binary in case of any problem, you can visit this link for more information:

http://docs.opencv.org/platforms/android/service/doc/UseCases.html#manager-selection

You should connect your Android device to your computer and make sure the **USB debugging** option is enabled. Then, in Eclipse right-click on the *OpenCV Tutorial-Camera Preview* application and select **Run** and Eclipse will create a pop-up for the first time. Then select **Android Application**. There will be a new pop-up for device selection. Select your device and keep calm. The OpenCV application will run on your Android device!

OpenCV4Android SDK is for the OpenCV Java API. You can see that codes are very similar to the C++ API. Java API documentation can be found at http://docs.opencv.org/java.

OpenCV has a huge community and support network. In case of need you can ask for support from http://opencv.org/support.html.

Summary

In this chapter, you learned about the basics of OpenCV and how to install it on your device. You also learned how to configure your OpenCV project on various platforms and in various development environments. After installing OpenCV, you ran your first OpenCV application!

OpenCV has huge support in terms of platform independency. We highly recommend you find out about OpenCV API's and the steadily increasing supported platforms. After setting up OpenCV in your favorite environment, you are ready for the next step!

The next chapter describes data acquisition with popular cameras that are widely used by both the robotics community and the OpenCV community.

3
Data Acquisition with OpenCV and Arduino

In this chapter you will learn about the data acquisition part of a computer vision system. Both the camera data and the sensor data will be handled. The chapter will teach you about camera and sensor selection in vision systems and the correct way to use them. Because of this, there are two main sections in this chapter; image and video acquisition with OpenCV and sensor data acquisition with Arduino.

Image and video acquisition

The visual representation of the environment for people is achieved vis eyes. When we talk about machines, various types of cameras are used for this purpose. Because it is a digital representation of the environment, efficient camera handling leads to better representation. This is something that you will learn from this chapter.

In *Chapter 2, Fundamentals and Installation of OpenCV*, you installed OpenCV and ran a typical "hello world" application. On top of this experience, we'll learn about the data acquisition capabilities of OpenCV by explaining the issues with hands-on practical examples.

OpenCV supports various types of cameras that give programmers a bigger set of choice. Learning how to select a camera for your application is one of the topics in this chapter. You'll get the answer to this question in the camera selection part of this chapter.

After selecting the camera, we'll instigate image and video acquisition by using OpenCV. In this process we'll look at how to read and write an image, video capture, and more! So, let's begin!

Camera selection

The camera selection issue is closely linked to the requirements and needs of the target application. So, take time at the start to consider in detail the system that you need. Later on, this simple step will save you time and money. In addition to these requirements, the capabilities of the camera should be considered. So, the link between application needs and camera capabilities should be very strong in order to make the best decision. This is exactly what this section stands for!

Resolution

To be able to pick the appropriate camera for an application, the necessary resolution and the relevant camera sensor properties are important, but the interpretation of the resolution term should be also clarified.

When we talk about a 2 megapixels (MP) camera, what does it mean? This refers purely to the number of pixels on the image (or a video frame). If the resulting image size or data of a particular camera is 1200 pixels height and 1800 pixels width, the image includes 1200x1800 = 2,160,000 pixels which is nearly 2 MP. Although this property is labeled as the resolution of the camera, normally for real life vision applications we need different information such as object resolution which is tightly bound to this information but requires more details.

In practice, resolution implies the measurement of the smallest possible distance between two points such that they can be perceived as separate from one another. Since the purpose of taking an image is capturing the details of an object or an event, the minimum size of details perceived in the object or the event is an important term for us. The same applies to videos, which are just a series of progressive images.

So, the important term; object resolution means the smallest detail of the object which we can sense via a camera. Because of this fact, the object and detail sizes are very important. The following formula shows the relation between a particular object, its size, and the details that can be acquired from it:

$$Object\ Resolution = \frac{Object\ Size\,(x*y)}{Minimum\ size\ of\ the\ object\ detail\ to\ be\ sensed\,(x*y)}$$

Let's give an example in a real life situation. Imagine that you want to read the license plate of a car. Assume that your camera sees only the full view of a car. The height and width of the car in front view is about 2 meters. And consider that, to be able to recognize the plate, you would need a detail which is 0.2 cm large and 0.2 cm long.

To understand the required object resolution of the car, we can put the values to the object resolution equation given as follows:

$$Resolution = \frac{200\,cm}{0.2\,cm} \times \frac{200\,cm}{0.2\,cm} = 1000 \times 1000 = 1MP$$

So we need a 1 MP resolution in this case. But please be aware that this calculation depends on the distance from the object to the camera. If we take the photo from far away, the object in the image will be smaller, so a higher camera resolution is needed to recognize the plate. The inverse situation is also valid. If the car is closer then the plate will be bigger in the image so that a lower camera resolution will suffice.

The relation between the distance and the resolution is a little bit complex but it can be simplified in a practical manner. This image is a great way to show the importance of the distance from the camera to the subject, as shown in the following diagram:

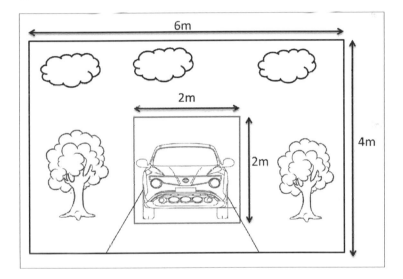

In this case we can easily say that the width is now three times and the height is now two times the car. So the total resolution is six times the initial calculation, and it is 6 MP, as shown in the following calculation:

$$Resolution = \frac{600\,cm}{0.2\,cm} \times \frac{400\,cm}{0.2\,cm} = 3000 \times 2000 = 6MP$$

The more you practice real life cases, the more precisely you will guess the required camera resolution for a specific application.

Color capabilities

There are two types of camera in terms of color capabilities; monochrome or color. The selection of color capabilities simply depends on the application. If the application requires color information, a color camera must be used. If color is not important but the shape is, it is logical to prefer a monochrome (grayscale) camera. Monochrome cameras are generally more sensitive than color cameras and deliver more detailed images. Combining these two is also possible and necessary in some cases.

Most webcams are color cameras. Moreover, by using OpenCV you can capture a grayscale image on them. Generally, to allow for expansion for future requirements, color cameras are preferred. In this way, you can extract both color and shape information.

Frame rate

Frame rate is measured in **Frames Per Second (FPS)**. The frame rate term describes the number of images that a camera can capture and transmit per second. Generally, webcams are up to 30 FPS. For some cameras, you can dynamically change the frame rate.

The higher the frame rate, the quicker the sensor. Moreover, a higher frame rate also leads to a higher use of data storage. Note that, if your application is not fast enough it might not be possible to fully exploit the actual FPS limits of the camera. If you want to find a product defect on a production line in a factory which produces 6,000 products per minute, probably you would need a high FPS camera. 6,000 products per minute means 100 products per second and, to be able to detect the defect assume that you would need 10 frames for each product and then you would need a 10*100=1000 FPS camera for this application.

The price is also higher for higher FPS cameras. Just make a heuristic calculation on the application needs as in the factory example and define your average need in terms of frame rate. For example, a good webcam may have a frame rate of 50 and the factory we were talking about in the previous paragraph requires at least a 1,000 FPS camera to detect defects so, if we make a quick calculation, we expect a 1,000 FPS camera to be 20 times more expensive than a good webcam.

2D or 3D

Because of their nature, cameras take a 2D (two dimensional) projection of the scene. Our webcams are 2D cameras so you are familiar with them.

3D cameras add the third dimension—the distance to the data. The term 3D camera may refer to a range camera or a stereo camera. A range camera produces a 2D image showing the distance of each pixel in a scene from a specific point. A stereo camera includes two aligned cameras which mimics the human vision and capture three dimensional images. By finding the shift amount of matching points in two images, it is possible to calculate the depth of any regions in the image.

If your application needs 3D capabilities, you can use a 3D camera such as Kinect, or Asus Xtion Pro Live. There are more!

Again, 3D data needs more storage. So, if you don't really need 3D information, carry on with 2D.

Communication interface

Communication interface affects lots of properties of the camera system. The popular interfaces are USB, FireWire, GigE and CameraLink. There are lots of parameters to compare but let's make a practical comparison table:

Interface	Cable Length	Max Bandwidth	Multi-Camera	Realtime	Plug and Play
USB 2.0	5 m	40 MB/s	Medium	Low	High
USB 3.0	8 m	350 MB/s	Medium	High	High
FireWire	4.5 m	65 MB/s	Medium	High	High
CameraLink	10 m	850 MB/s	Low	High	Low
GigE	100 m	100 MB/s	High	Medium	Medium

As can be seen from the table, the communication interface highly impacts the camera distance from the controller, bandwidth, FPS and even usability! So, please evaluate your needs and pick the proper interface for your application.

Webcams have a USB interface. So they have a fair cable length, bandwidth, FPS, and usability. Adding in their accessibility, it makes sense to use webcams with most computer vision applications.

Image acquisition

Up till now, we have built a solid background for an efficient camera selection process. Now it is time to go one step further; reading data from the camera.

Since simplicity is the ultimate sophistication, it is beneficial to keep everything practical and easy to apply. Because of this, our examples will be over a standard webcam. Logitech C120 is used as the webcam in the example applications. Please be aware that camera drivers should be installed to be able to work with OpenCV.

The OpenCV C++ API is used to read data from a camera. Moreover, OpenCV has great documentation so it is really easy to convert the examples to C, Python or Java API. You may want to visit opencv.org for further information.

Reading a static image

It is beneficial to work on sample static images for the proof of concept phase of the design. For instance, imagine that you want to develop a face recognition application. Firstly, you should work on a sample set of face images. So, reading a static image from the data storage would be the first step in this process.

OpenCV really makes computer vision easy! Let's take advantage of the power of OpenCV and read a static image from the storage. Now, we'll write a code that reads a static image and displays it in a window. Please write the following code to your OpenCV development environment and save it as read_static_image.cpp:

```cpp
#include <opencv2/core/core.hpp>
#include <opencv2/highgui/highgui.hpp>
#include <iostream>

using namespace cv;
using namespace std;

int main( int argc, char** argv )
{
    if( argc != 2)
    {
    cout <<" Usage: read_static_image    lena.jpg" << endl;
      return -1;
    }

    Mat image;
    // Read the image file name
    image = imread(argv[1], CV_LOAD_IMAGE_COLOR);
```

```
    // Check for invalid input
    if( image.data == NULL )
    {
        cout <<  "Couldn't open the image" << endl ;
        return -1;
    }
    // Create a window for display.
    namedWindow( "Read Static Image", WINDOW_AUTOSIZE );
    //Display the image
    imshow( "Read Static Image", image );
    // Wait for a keystroke in the window
    waitKey(0);
    return 0;
}
```

When you compile this code, it will produce an executable. In Windows, let's say it is read_static_image.exe. For the input image, you can use a very famous image in computer vision lena.jpg. For Windows, copy the lena.jpg file under C:/cv_book/. In the cmd.exe window, navigate to the directory which includes read_static_image.exe. The command should be similar to:

```
read_static_image C:/cv_book/lena.jpg
```

It is more or less same for other platforms. For example, if your executable is read_static_image.exe and the image file lena.jpg is in the same folder you can run the application using the following command:

```
./read_static_image lena.jpg
```

Now let's explain the code. The basic parts include headers that have already been explained in the previous chapter. Let's continue from the new section, as shown in the following code snippet:

```
if( argc != 2)
{
cout <<" Usage: read_static_image    image_filename.jpg" << endl;
return -1;
}
```

Firstly we check if the arguments are okay. As you see from the preceding command lines, there should be two arguments: the first argument is the program itself and the second argument is the image path. If the argument number is different from 2, the program prints a help text and exits with an error.

In the next step, a `Mat` object is created to store image data and, by using an image path, image data is read in a RGB color format, as shown here:

```
Mat image;
// Read the image file name
image = imread(argv[1], CV_LOAD_IMAGE_COLOR);
```

We then check if the image has been successfully read and if the image data is not empty. A window is created with the name `Read Static Image` and the image is shown in that window.

```
If(image.data == NULL)
{
cout << "Couldn't open the image" << endl;
return 1;
}
namedWindow( "Read Static Image", WINDOW_AUTOSIZE );
    imshow( "Read Static Image", image );
```

We want the image to be displayed until a key press so we use the `waitKey` function whose only parameter is how long it (in milliseconds) should wait for user input. Zero means to wait forever:

```
waitKey(0);
```

The output of the program is shown here:

You can use the CV_LOAD_IMAGE_GRAYSCALE property to load the image in grayscale format!

```
image = imread(argv[1], CV_LOAD_IMAGE_GRAYSCALE);
```

Taking a snapshot from a webcam

Sometimes it is necessary to take a snapshot from the camera and save it to the storage for further analysis. This process generally starts with a trigger.

Remember our face recognition-based door lock example. When the visitor pushes the bell button, the system takes a snapshot of the face and analyzes it for the face recognition process. This application is a good example of a snapshot operation. It is possible to find similar situations so let's take a snapshot from the camera. Create a project with the following code and save the code as take_snapshot.cpp.

```cpp
#include <opencv2/core/core.hpp>
#include <opencv2/highgui/highgui.hpp>
#include <iostream>

using namespace cv;
using namespace std;

int main( int argc, char** argv )
{
  if( argc != 2)
    {
    cout <<" Usage: take_snapshot snapshot.jpg" << endl;
        return -1;
    }
  //create the capture object
  VideoCapture cap(CV_CAP_ANY);

  // Get the frame
  Mat frame;
  cap >> frame;
  //Check if frame is empty or not
  if(frame.empty())
  {
    cerr << "Could not get frame from camera" << endl;
    return -1;
  }
  // Save the frame into a file
  imwrite(argv[1], frame);

  return 0;
}
```

The preceding code is very similar to the `read_static_image.cpp` file. However, it only reads one frame from the camera and saves the frame with the name which is taken from the command line argument. The Windows command line is shown here:

```
take_snapshot snapshot.jpg
```

If your application name is different from `take_snaphot`, replace `take_snapshot` with your application name when you try to run it. Now let's explain the code!

We initially created a video capture object which can capture data from any connected camera using the following line. Normally, the `CV_CAP_ANY` value corresponds to a `0` value. If you have more than one attached camera you can manually increase the index, as in `cap(1)`:

```
VideoCapture cap(CV_CAP_ANY);
```

Now, for the next step, we create a matrix for storing the frame and read one frame from the `cap` object:

```
Mat frame;
cap >> frame;
```

After checking if the frame is not empty, and thus read, we save the image by using the `imwrite` function. The filename of the image frame is taken from command line argument number one.

```
imwrite(argv[1], frame);
```

Getting a video stream from the webcam

Video processing applications generally need a video stream as the input data. By investigating the inter-frame information, it becomes possible to accomplish higher level tasks such as motion recognition.

The FPS value of the video stream and the resolution become very important in this process because they directly affect real time behavior. Higher FPS values mean that you have less time to complete processing. Similarly, higher resolution increases the calculation complexity and time.

Hand gesture-based motion detection is a good use case for video streaming. Similarly, a line follower robot should also capture a real time video stream to be able to continuously follow the line. So, as long as we understand the importance of the topic, let's capture this live video stream, using this code:

```
#include <opencv/cv.h>
#include <opencv/highgui.h>
#include <iostream>
```

```cpp
using namespace cv;
using namespace std;

void ProcessFrame(Mat& newFrame)
{
  cvtColor(newFrame, newFrame, CV_BGR2GRAY);
}

int main( int argc, char** argv )
{
  //create the capture object
  VideoCapture cap(CV_CAP_ANY);

  while(1)
  {
    // Get the frame
    Mat frame;
    cap >> frame;
    //Check if frame is empty or not
    if(frame.empty())
    {
      cerr << " could not get frame." << endl;
      return -1;
    }
    ProcessFrame(frame);
    imshow("Live vide stream",frame);
    if(waitKey(30) >= 0) break;
  }
  return 0;
}
```

The code is very similar to the snapshot code except that the frame read process is now inside an infinite `while` loop. There is an optional `ProcessFrame` function which converts the video frames to grayscale. If you want the frames in full color, comment the `ProcessFrame` function.

> When running the code, you can see a live video stream from your camera!
>
> To change the FPS of your stream, you can use the function given here `bool VideoCapture::set(int propId, double value)` with propId `CV_CAP_PROP_FPS`. To change the FPS to 10 FPS you can type:
>
>   cap.set(CV_CAP_PROP_FPS,10);
>
> Do not forget to check if your camera supports different frame rates.

Interaction with Kinect

Kinect is a revolutionary 3D imaging device, developed by Microsoft and widely used in many computer vision applications. The first version of Kinect was distributed with the popular gaming console Xbox 360 and the newer version was announced with Xbox One. Although it was originally created for gaming, Kinect hugely improves 3D computer vision applications!

Kinect's default connector was specially designed for Xbox and both power and data signals are carried via the same cable. To be able to use the Kinect with your PC or microcomputer, you need to have a USB convertor cable:

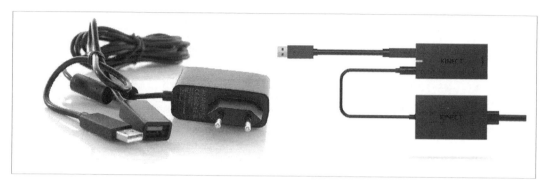

Now let's interact with Kinect and access it with OpenCV. Then you will be ready for 3D vision applications!

Integration of Kinect with OpenCV

Installing **Point Cloud Library (PCL)** will install all the software and drivers needed for Kinect. PCL is a multiplatform library. You can install PCL from http://pointclouds.org/. For the Mac, you don't need to install PCL to use Kinect. Just follow the chapter and you will get your Kinect working.

You need to install the libfreenect driver to make Kinect work with OpenCV. Now let's jump into this topic! We'll do this example on a Mac, but it will work in the same way on other platforms.

Installing on a Mac

It is better to install with a package manager such as Homebrew, Macports, or Fink. As we did before, we will use Homebrew for the installation.

Let's follow these steps to install `libfreenect`:

1. If you don't have Homebrew, you can check for instructions in the *Installation of OpenCV on Mac OS* section in *Chapter 2, Fundamentals and Installation of OpenCV*. Whether you had Homebrew or not, run the following command to update Homebrew:

   ```
   brew update
   ```

2. To install `libfreenect`, type this command into the terminal:

   ```
   brew install libfreenect
   ```

3. That's all, now you can plug your Kinect into your computer and run the executable given here, to experience depth in an image:

   ```
   freenect-glview
   ```

Xcode integration

As with the OpenCV integration with Xcode, we will follow similar steps to integrate `libfreenect` in order to use the Kinect capabilities in OpenCV.

1. Follow the steps we used for the `OpenCV_Template` project in the previous chapter for the new project. Name it `OpeCV_Kinect`.

2. Click on the `OpenCV_Kinect` project | **Build Settings** | **Search Paths** | **Header Search Paths** and click (**+**) to add the two paths given here:

   ```
   /usr/local/include/libusb-1.0
   /usr/local/include/libfreenect
   ```

3. Then, click on **Build Phases** | **Link Binary with Libraries** and click (**+**) to add the two required frameworks:

   ```
   GLUT.framework
   OpenGL.framework
   ```

4. After adding the frameworks, we need to add the `libfreenect` and `libusb` libraries. Again, click (**+**) then click on **Add Other...**.

5. Press (*cmd* + *Shift* + *g*) then type `/usr/local/lib` in the pop-up window. After that, select `libfreenect_*.dylibs`. Keep pressing the `cmd` button while selecting.

6. Now, let's perform the same procedure to add the `libusb` libraries. Press *cmd* + *Shift* + *g*, then type `/usr/local/lib` in the pop-up window. Then, select `libusb*.dylibs`.

That's all for integration! We are ready to move on to coding. Follow these steps:

1. Download `libfreenect-master` for accessing the source codes which we will use. You can download it from `https://github.com/OpenKinect/libfreenect`.

2. Copy and paste the code given in `libfreenect-master/wrappers/opencv/cvdemo.c` to your `main.cpp` in your `OpenCV_Kinect` project.

3. Lastly, we need to drag and drop `libfreenect_cv.h` and `libfreenect_cv.c` to the `OpenCV_Kinect` folder (the folder where the `main.cpp` is) and build it! The following is the code for `main.cpp`:

```cpp
#include <opencv/cv.h>
#include <opencv/highgui.h>
#include <stdio.h>
#include "libfreenect_cv.h"

IplImage *GlViewColor(IplImage *depth)
{
  static IplImage *image = 0;
  if (!image) image = cvCreateImage(cvSize(640,480), 8, 3);
  unsigned char *depth_mid = (unsigned char*)(image->imageData);
  int i;
  for (i = 0; i < 640*480; i++) {
    int lb = ((short *)depth->imageData)[i] % 256;
    int ub = ((short *)depth->imageData)[i] / 256;
    switch (ub) {
      case 0:
        depth_mid[3*i+2] = 255;
        depth_mid[3*i+1] = 255-lb;
        depth_mid[3*i+0] = 255-lb;
        break;
      case 1:
        depth_mid[3*i+2] = 255;
        depth_mid[3*i+1] = lb;
        depth_mid[3*i+0] = 0;
        break;
      case 2:
        depth_mid[3*i+2] = 255-lb;
        depth_mid[3*i+1] = 255;
        depth_mid[3*i+0] = 0;
        break;
      case 3:
        depth_mid[3*i+2] = 0;
```

```
            depth_mid[3*i+1] = 255;
            depth_mid[3*i+0] = lb;
            break;
          case 4:
            depth_mid[3*i+2] = 0;
            depth_mid[3*i+1] = 255-lb;
            depth_mid[3*i+0] = 255;
            break;
          case 5:
            depth_mid[3*i+2] = 0;
            depth_mid[3*i+1] = 0;
            depth_mid[3*i+0] = 255-lb;
            break;
          default:
            depth_mid[3*i+2] = 0;
            depth_mid[3*i+1] = 0;
            depth_mid[3*i+0] = 0;
            break;
        }
    }
    return image;
}

int main(int argc, char **argv)
{
    while (cvWaitKey(10) < 0) {
        IplImage *image = freenect_sync_get_rgb_cv(0);
        if (!image) {
            printf("Error: Kinect not connected?\n");
            return -1;
        }
        cvCvtColor(image, image, CV_RGB2BGR);
        IplImage *depth = freenect_sync_get_depth_cv(0);
        if (!depth) {
            printf("Error: Kinect not connected?\n");
            return -1;
        }
        cvShowImage("RGB", image);
        cvShowImage("Depth", GlViewColor(depth));
    }
    return 0;
}
```

Now let's go through the code and explain what is going on to make it work and get the depth image from Kinect:

```
IplImage *GlViewColor(IplImage *depth)
{
  static IplImage *image = 0;
  if (!image) image = cvCreateImage(cvSize(640,480), 8, 3);
  unsigned char *depth_mid = (unsigned char*)(image->imageData);
  int i;
  for (i = 0; i < 640*480; i++) {
    int lb = ((short *)depth->imageData)[i] % 256;
    int ub = ((short *)depth->imageData)[i] / 256;
    switch (ub) {
      case 0:
        depth_mid[3*i+2] = 255;
        depth_mid[3*i+1] = 255-lb;
        depth_mid[3*i+0] = 255-lb;
        break;
      case 1:
        depth_mid[3*i+2] = 255;
        depth_mid[3*i+1] = lb;
        depth_mid[3*i+0] = 0;
        break;
      case 2:
        depth_mid[3*i+2] = 255-lb;
        depth_mid[3*i+1] = 255;
        depth_mid[3*i+0] = 0;
        break;
      case 3:
        depth_mid[3*i+2] = 0;
        depth_mid[3*i+1] = 255;
        depth_mid[3*i+0] = lb;
        break;
      case 4:
        depth_mid[3*i+2] = 0;
        depth_mid[3*i+1] = 255-lb;
        depth_mid[3*i+0] = 255;
        break;
      case 5:
        depth_mid[3*i+2] = 0;
        depth_mid[3*i+1] = 0;
        depth_mid[3*i+0] = 255-lb;
        break;
      default:
```

```
            depth_mid[3*i+2] = 0;
            depth_mid[3*i+1] = 0;
            depth_mid[3*i+0] = 0;
            break;
        }
    }
    return image;
}
```

The data coming from Kinect needed to be converted into an appropriate format in order to store depth data. In the `for` loop of the `IplImage *GlViewColor(IplImage *depth)` function, depth information is converted into colors. This function returns a scaled image for representation. This is the code body of the `main` function:

```
int main(int argc, char **argv)
{
    while (cvWaitKey(10) < 0) {
        IplImage *image = freenect_sync_get_rgb_cv(0);
        if (!image) {
            printf("Error: Kinect not connected?\n");
            return -1;
        }
        cvCvtColor(image, image, CV_RGB2BGR);
        IplImage *depth = freenect_sync_get_depth_cv(0);
        if (!depth) {
            printf("Error: Kinect not connected?\n");
            return -1;
        }
        cvShowImage("RGB", image);
        cvShowImage("Depth", GlViewColor(depth));
    }
    return 0;
}
```

In the `main` function, we have a `while` loop which polls unless any key press comes from the keyboard. The `while` loop runs every 10 milliseconds because `cvWaitKey(10)` is dictated to wait 10 milliseconds:

```
IplImage *image = freenect_sync_get_rgb_cv(0);
        if (!image) {
            printf("Error: Kinect not connected?\n");
            return -1;
        }
    cvCvtColor(image, image, CV_RGB2BGR);
```

The `Libfreenect` function, `freenect_sync_get_rgb_cv`, receives the RGB camera image and loads it to the `IplImage *` image pointer, as shown in the following code. The *if* statement in the code checks whether the image is correct or not, otherwise, it returns `-1` to terminate the program. With the help of the `cvCvtColor` function, the image is reorganized from the RGB format to the BGR format:

```
IplImage *depth = freenect_sync_get_depth_cv(0);
        if (!depth) {
            printf("Error: Kinect not connected?\n");
            return -1;
        }
```

A similar process is carried out for depth information. The `freenect_sync_get_depth_cv` function gets the depth raw map and puts it into the `IplImage *depth` pointer. Then, a check is made to see whether the depth image is loaded or not. These are the lines after the `if` loop:

```
cvShowImage("RGB", image);
cvShowImage("Depth", GlViewColor(depth));
```

Now it is time to represent images in both RGB and depth. If you look closely at the second line in the previous code snippet, you will see that the raw depth image is given inside the `GlViewColor` function for scaling.

When you successfully run the code, you will see the following screenshots:

You can see that objects nearer to the camera are redder and the distant ones are greener.

Sensor data acquisition

In most real-time applications, the combination of vision information and sensor information is essential to get a wider sense of the environment. As the overall performance of the system is tightly bound to all sub-blocks, efficient and proper implementation of sensor acquisition becomes very important.

Even to detect the same physical object, there are lots of different sensors. As a simple example, there are many types of temperature sensors, although they are all designed to measure temperature. If you want to measure skin temperature but not the atmosphere, how do you choose the right sensor? How do you pick a sampling interval? How do you deal with noises? This chapter aims to give you a thorough understanding of sensor data acquisition. At the end of the chapter there are real life sensor interfacing examples which were developed with Arduino Uno R3.

Setting up an Arduino environment

As it was explained earlier, Arduino is a perfect platform for fast prototyping of embedded system applications. In the right context, it is also a perfect tool for sensor data collection with its huge library and community support.

To be able to develop Arduino applications, you need to download Arduino IDE from the official Arduino website (http://arduino.cc/en/Main/Software). In this book, Arduino Uno R3 is used for all the applications. But the same basic principles are valid for all other Arduino platforms. The following is a typical Arduino IDE screenshot:

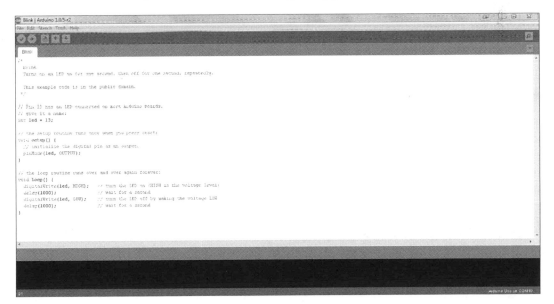

Just grab your Arduino Uno R3, download the Arduino IDE and set up the environment. This procedure is as straightforward as installing any other application. Then you will be ready for action!

Fundamentals of sensors

It is important to know the fundamentals of sensors to fully understand the sensor interfacing issue. In this section, basic sensor classifications, sampling theorem and methods for dealing with sensor noises are discussed. You will learn a lot about sensors and how to use them efficiently in your vision application.

Sensor types

There is a nearly infinite number of sensor types, but even so, it is possible to make meaningful classifications to generalize the process of choice.

The most basic classification is the physical parameter which tends to be measured. Temperature, light level, pressure, acceleration and humidity are examples of such physical parameters. Even though there are lots of physical parameters, the interfacing is similar for most of them. Once you get this idea and practice enough, it is not a problem to measure most physical parameters.

Sensors can be classified into two categories according to output signal type: analog sensors and digital sensors. While analog sensors give continuous information, digital sensors give discrete information.

Because nearly all embedded systems can be classified as digital systems, the sensor data should be in digital format to be processed by the embedded system in any case. Because of this, all analog sensors are interfaced via a special peripheral **Analog to Digital Convertor (ADC)**. This makes our lives very simple; using more or less the same software you can read a light sensor in the same way you read a temperature sensor. The interpretation of the read data is, of course, different.

Digital sensors are generally accessed via the same embedded communication interfaces (peripherals) such as the **Universal Synchronous and Asynchronous Receiver/Transmitter (USART)**, the **Inter Integrated Circuit (I2C)** or the **Serial Peripheral Interface (SPI)**. By accessing special memory regions called registers, it is possible to configure the sensor and read the data inside it. So, digital sensors generally give more options on configuration. Because of this, complex sensors such as motion sensors are designed with a digital interface. The best news is that, once you learn about these communication interfaces, it is more or less the same when using different types of sensors! Note that the Arduino IDE provides libraries to interface with these types of communication which often makes these sensors easier to use.

So, get ready to learn! In the next step, two important topics on sensor data reading will be covered: sampling rate and noise suppressions.

Sampling theorem

Sampling of sensor data defines the sampling rate of the data reads from the sensor. If you need to sample a sensor in real time, how often do you sample the input? Would a sampling process of every 50 ms or 100 ms be sufficient? How do you determine the best rate of sampling? One of the simple answers is to try some sample rates and decide on the best one! But, of course, this can often fail.

In signal processing, the Nyquist criterion is used to determine the sampling rate. The Nyquist criterion simply states that the sampling rate must be at least twice as fast as the highest frequency component in the input signal. Given such a sampling rate, it would be possible to reconstruct the original input signal without losing the information carried by the original input signal. This approach is good when you know the maximum frequency component of a signal. Even in that case, it is safer to sample data five times faster than the maximum frequency of the signal.

But, in general, it is impossible or too hard to define the maximum frequency component of the sensor data. So, an educated guess is usually better when choosing a sampling sensor. We are lucky that digital sensors generally solve this sampling problem by considering the purpose of the sensor. But the same is not true for analog sensors and, in that case, you have to pick a sampling rate by considering the limitations. One option is to select the highest possible sampling rate but this is not a good idea because it will lead to much more data power consumption, storage needs, and computation time so it will adversely affect everything we want to protect. So, there must be another way of approaching this problem.

Imagine that you want to sample the temperature data of the atmosphere. It is not normal for the temperature of a room to change 10 degrees in Celsius in one second. Sampling once every 10 seconds won't affect anything in most cases as in the context of this sample application. But if we want to sample an accelerometer to detect movement, for example, we should look at the fastest movement to be detected which might be a hand gesture of two seconds' duration. To be able to separate the gesture pattern you would probably need 200 samples from the movement and $2/200 = 10$ ms for the sampling rate (which is equivalent to 100 Hz) is a good start point for this example. By using this simple process it would be possible to ascertain the best sampling rate.

Dealing with noise

If we need to capture data from a sensor, noises arrive with the actual measurement. In practice it is impossible to completely remove noise, but it is possible to reduce the noise ratio to an acceptable rate. The noise tolerance of a medical application naturally would be less than with a hobby application. Do not forget that the acceptable level of noise is entirely dependent on the application.

The war against sensor noise starts with the electrical interfacing of the sensor. Hopefully, each manufacturer has put a sample driving circuit in the sensor's user manual or datasheet. Follow this reference design unless you have a fantastic interface design in mind to change the rules of the game.

Another way of dealing with noise is a filtering process to remove the noisy part from the sensor data. As in the sampling rate selection process, application context affects the filtering process of sensor data. For instance, if you are dealing with a temperature sensor, you can simply remove the high frequency data that is noise. This is because it is not logical to expect a 10 degree change in one second. Similarly, for motion detection, you can remove the excessively high and low frequency components from your application.

Noise suppression can be managed with hardware or software based solutions. A hardware-based approach can be achieved with extra components on the circuit. On the other hand, a software-based approach can be achieved with coding. The hardware-based approach is generally used when you need very fast filtering but it will cost more. Most of the time it is not feasible to change the hardware and it is generally easier and more flexible to use software-based noise suppression.

Because embedded systems generally have a limited amount of resources, we cannot apply very complex filters to embedded systems. But this does not mean that it is impossible to apply effective filters to such systems. In the next two examples you will see some filtering implementations which are quite simple and effective.

Reading data from the temperature sensor

As you have enough knowledge for hands-on practice, it would be good to start by reading a relatively simple analog sensor.

LM35 series are precision centigrade temperature sensors with an output voltage linearly proportional to the Centigrade scale. The LM35 device does not require any external calibration or trimming to give an accuracy of of 0.25 degrees celcius at room temperature and 0.75 degrees celcius over a full -55 degrees celcius to 150 degrees celcius temperature range.

You do not need much equipment to set up the sensor data acquisition system for the LM35. Just grab the Arduino Uno R3 module, the LM35 device, a breadboard, some connecting wires and your computer! Do not forget that many other sensors work with a similar architecture. Distance sensors, light sensors, and anything that outputs 0 to 5V can be read in a similar fashion.

The LM35 device has three pins—GND, +VS, and VOUT. Firstly, by using connection cables, connect the +Vs to +5 V on your Arduino Uno R3. Secondly, connect VOUT to Analog0 (or A0) on the Arduino board. And, as the last step, connect GND to GND on the Arduino Uno R3. This connection is shown in the following diagram. In this configuration, the LM25 device can only measure positive temperatures:

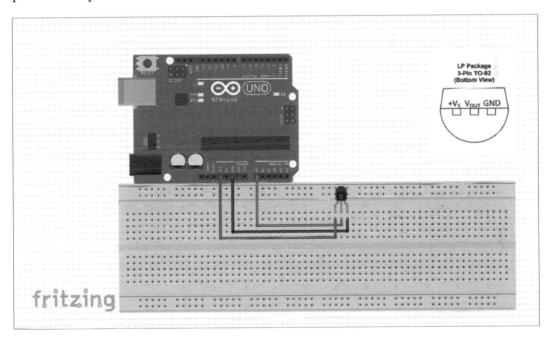

As we mentioned before, analog sensors should be interfaced via ADC. The Arduino Uno R3 has a 10-bit ADC. By using 10-bits it is possible to write $2^{10}=1024$ numbers. This means ADC can divide its reference voltage 5 V to 1024 pieces. In this case 5.0 V is mapped to the ADC value 1023 and 2.50 V is mapped to 512, for example. So, ADC sampled voltage can be calculated, as shown here:

$$V_{SAMPLE} = ADC_{SAMPLE} * \frac{5V}{1024}$$

ADCSAMPLE is the value which you read from the ADC module. According to this simple formula, if you read the ADCSAMPLE value as 135, for example, the voltage on the pin should be:

$$V_{SAMPLE} = 135 * \frac{5V}{1024} = 0.66V = 660\,mV$$

As is specified in the LM35 datasheet, each 10 mV corresponds to 1 degree celcuis. Hence $660\,mV$ indicates a temperature of 66 degrees celsius. So let's paste the following code in the Arduino IDE and download it to the Arduino Uno R3:

```
#define TEMPERATURE_SENSOR_ADC (0)
float temperatureInCelcius=0.0;

void setup()
{
  Serial.begin(9600);
}

void loop()
{
  temperatureInCelcius = (analogRead(TEMPERATURE_SENSOR_ADC) *
5.0) / (1024.0 * 10.0);
  Serial.print("TEMPRATURE = ");
  Serial.print(temperatureInCelcius);
  Serial.print("*C");
  Serial.println();
  delay(1000);
}
```

After compiling the code and downloading it to your Arduino Uno R3, when connecting the Arduino over a USB serial terminal you will see the temperature values. As you can see, we sample the sensor once every second.

But the problem is still not solved. You can see that the maximum temperature measured by the LM35 is 150 degree celcius meaning that the maximum possible output voltage is 1.50 V. It means that we are wasting the 5 V interval by not using the full range. So, the current resolution plan is not well organized. A room temperature of 150 degree celcius is again not so useful. A smarter approach can be found.

If we change the analog reference voltage (which was 5.0 V in the first case) to a lower value such as 1.1 V, it is possible to increase the measurement resolution. In this case the formula would change, as shown here:

$$Temperature = \frac{\left(ADC_{SAMPLE} * \dfrac{1100mV}{1024} \right)}{10mV} = \frac{ADC_{SAMPLE}}{9.31}$$

To change the analog reference to 1.1 V, the `analogReference(INTERNAL);` function command is used. We can also apply a simple filtering algorithm to surpass the high frequency changes. Such an implementation can be found in the second version of our LM35 read code, as shown here:

```
#define TEMPERATURE_SENSOR_ADC (0)
float temperatureInCelcOld=0.0;
float temperatureInCelcNew=0.0;
float filterCoeff = 0.1;

void setup()
{
  Serial.begin(9600);
  analogReference(INTERNAL);
  temperatureInCelcNew = analogRead(TEMPERATURE_SENSOR_ADC) /
9.31;
  temperatureInCelcOld = temperatureInCelcNew;
}

void loop()
{
  temperatureInCelcNew = analogRead(TEMPERATURE_SENSOR_ADC) /
9.31;
  temperatureInCelcNew = ((1.0 -filterCoeff) *
temperatureInCelcNew) + (filterCoeff * temperatureInCelcOld);
  temperatureInCelcOld = temperatureInCelcNew;
  Serial.print("TEMPRATURE = ");
  Serial.print(temperatureInCelcNew);
  Serial.print("*C");
  Serial.println();
  delay(1000);
}
```

Probably the most important part is the filtering formula. Basically, the filter which is applied in the code is known as a boxcar integrator. The general shape of the filter implementation is as follows:

```
current_output = (1 -a) * input + a * previous_output, 0 < a < 1.0
```

In the preceding formula, the new filtered temperature value (`current_output`) is determined by using %90 of the new temperature value (`input`) and %10 of the old temperature value. Hence, noisy high frequency temperature movements are %10 suppressed by the effect of the old sample.

Additionally, by using a 1.1 V region we now have higher resolution temperature information. Do not forget that, in that case, the maximum temperature is 110 degrees celcius, which is also acceptable. In conclusion, we now have much better sensor interfacing.

 Please analyze the Arduino sensor examples and try to guess how they could be improved in terms of the know-how you acquired in this chapter. You will see that the same principles can be easily applied to all kinds of sensor applications!

Summary

By now, we know how to deal with data acquisition in vision projects. Now you know how to select a camera for a specific computer vision application. You also know how to capture data by using OpenCV for different acquisition needs.

After reading this chapter you also know how to read sensor data, how to use sensors and how to use filtering on sensor data. All of these topics were covered for different types of sensors so you now have a good understanding of data acquisition for computer vision applications.

Now, it is time to take the next step: filtering data with OpenCV!

Filtering Data with OpenCV

4

At this point, we have enough knowledge to go one step further. You understood the fundamentals of OpenCV, and data acquisition with OpenCV and Arduino. You now know that these methods require the manipulation of images we get from cameras. It is time to learn how to manipulate images to exploit the benefits of image filtering. After that, we will go through more sophisticated methods. This chapter introduces the practical usage of OpenCV filtering operations and, at the end of the chapter, we will work on a comprehensive project. In this chapter, you'll make your data ready to process!

Getting started with filtering

As a first step in image filtering, we will introduce image noise suppression, enhancement and other preprocessing methods. Operations covered in this chapter will give us a solid base for more post image processing and recognition that we will cover in later chapters.

Let's start with filters by looking at real life examples! There are plenty of industry applications for the filters and operations that we will discuss in this chapter. For instance, we can create a coin separator robot application which separates coins on a conveyor belt by implementing smoothing, sharpening and, lastly, morphological operators, to identify coins. As you will see, these operators reveal structures and shapes in an image.

2D convolution

Convolution is a fundamental operator that performs a shift and sum operation on an image. Convolution is a summation that declares the amount of overlap of one function as it is shifted through another function. It blends one function or image with another. This can be used to perform many practical operations on images such as smoothing, sharpening, feature extraction, and variation. As you will see in the next chapter, we will blend kernels (2D arrays, just like images) with images.

In practice, convolution is used to apply various kinds of filters in image processing. The mathematical element that is shifted over an image to perform convolution is a matrix generally known as a kernel. We can design our own kernel to satisfy implementation-specific needs. For instance, a kernel can be constructed to blur the image and another kernel can be constructed for edge detection. A blurring kernel and an edge detection kernel are given as follows:

Blurring kernel:

1/9	1/9	1/9
1/9	1/9	1/9
1/9	1/9	1/9

Edge detection kernel:

0	-1	0
-1	4	-1
0	-1	0

Convolution is a local and linear operation. It produces output pixel values based on the pixel values in its neighborhood, as determined by the kernel. It is important to understand the behavior of the convolution rather than its mathematical expression. Convolution is used to apply filters or signals to systems. Because image data is 2D, 2D convolution is used.

Spatial domain filtering

We will talk about the spatial domain in this chapter. Filtering in the spatial domain works on the image plane itself. Operations in this domain are based on direct manipulation of the pixels at their own location. In other words, operations take place on the pixels where we see on the screen.

Let's describe the spatial filters that we will discuss in this section of the chapter. Mainly, we will be talking about smoothing and sharpening. When we **smooth** an image, the operation tends to diminish corners, edges, and more importantly, noise spikes. Transitions on the image become smoother. The blurring operation is commonly applied to images to diminish the effect of noises on the image.

Sharpening has the opposite effect of smoothing; sharpening is another important filtering technique that is applied for enhancing corners and edges on the image. When using a sharpening filter, transitions on the image are exaggerated. With the help of this operation you get a better appreciation of previously soft transitions on the image.

Linear image filtering using convolution is the most common method of processing images. Tasks such as smoothing, sharpening, and edge finding are typical examples of image processing tasks that have convolution-based implementations which are linear.

For more information about linear filters you can read the Wikipedia page here https://en.wikipedia.org/wiki/Linear_filter.

Smoothing

Blurring or smoothing is a widely used processing operation in image processing. As we mentioned before, one of the most important operations is to suppress noise in the images. Another important usage of blurring is that it takes place when we need to reduce the resolution of an image. However, we will not cover resolution manipulation in this chapter. The following picture shows blurring and smoothing effects:

The series of images that are shown here give the effect of kernel size variations. Bigger kernels have bigger effects on images.

Now let's look closer to the OpenCV smoothing function that is carried out with one of the dedicated functions, the `GaussianBlur` function. This is the typical argument that the `GaussianBlur` function accepts:

```
GaussianBlur(frameIn, frameOut, Size(7,7), 1.5, 1.5);
```

It would be a good start if we explained each argument of the `GaussianBlur` function. Note that the functions that we will introduce in this chapter take very similar arguments. Other than filter-specific arguments, source, destination, and kernel size are given in the same sequence to all the OpenCV filter functions. The first argument is the picture that we are passing to the function, and the second argument is the image that will be returned by the function. Each has to be declared before the function is called, and it is possible that both can be the same thing. This will just overwrite the original image with the new one. Then, kernel dimensions are given to the function. `GaussianBlur`-specific arguments such as standard deviations in x and y directions are also given to the function.

 For more information about Gaussian distribution you can read the Wikipedia page here `https://en.wikipedia.org/wiki/Normal_distribution`.

Sharpening

Sharpening is an operation typically used to increase the visual sharpness of the image. In other words, it removes blurring and increases the focus of blurry regions. It therefore enhances local details.

For sharpening, we need to amplify the transitions on the image that will lead us to find edges in the image, as shown in this picture:

The original and the sharpened images are shown in the preceding picture. If we look closer we can see that the image on the right is sharper than the image on the left. To sharpen an image, we use the following lines of code:

```
GaussianBlur(frameIn,frameBlurred, Size(5,5), 5, 5);
addWeighted(frameIn, 1.5, frameBlurred, -0.5, 0, frameOut);
```

We use the same blurring operation as before, then subtract the `frameBlurred` component from the `frameIn` image. It has the effect of removing some of the blurring that may have occurred when the image was taken. The sharpened image is written to the `frameOut` image.

Color conversions

We use color conversion for better information representations. Some major color spaces supported in OpenCV are **blue, green, red (BGR)**, **hue, saturation and brightness (HSB)**, grayscale, and binary. The most frequently used color model is the BGR color scheme. Blue, green and red are primary colors and their combinations represent full color images.

The HSB (also known as **hue**, **saturation**, **value** or **HSV**) model separates color information from luminance. Hue represents the dominant color as seen by the observer, saturation refers to the amount of dilution of the color with white light, and brightness defines the average luminance. HSB representation is frequently used in color image processing because hue is relatively independent from light intensity. It is used to detect an object with a known color. HSB representation works in different lighting conditions! This is difficult to do with BGR values.

Grayscale is another frequently used color space where image information is given in shades of grey. The gray color occurs when the red, green and blue values of a pixel are the same. Because the value of each color is the same, we can use this single value to represent the grayscale value.

Binary operations create a two-level version of an image whose pixel values correspond to 0s and 1s. It typically enhances the contrast and is used for feature detection, image segmentation or as a processing step prior to the application of other image processing functions. It is best to apply this when all foreground pixels have higher intensity values than the background pixels.

One example of a binary operation is thresholding, which is a point-based operation that assigns the value of pixels to 0s or 1s by making a comparison with the global cut-off value.

The thresholding operation simply compares each pixel value in a grayscale image with a threshold and, if the pixel value is greater than the threshold, the pixel value is 1 and if the pixel value is less than the threshold, the pixel value is 0, and vice versa. The idea of thresholding can also be applied to BGR, HSV, and even depth data images. It is a useful way to pick out pixels in the image with a specific property but we will not cover these topics. Binary images permit the use of powerful morphological operators for the shape and structure-based analysis of images.

Grayscale

We convert our image into grayscale when we don't need the color information. The second reason is that some operations only accept grayscale images, such as the threshold function. The `cvtColor` function helps to convert image models from one to another. It is used as shown here:

```
cvtColor(frameIn, frameInGray, CV_BGR2GRAY);
```

The following picture is the result of using the cvtColor function:

Basically, the cvtColor function takes a 3-channel image, BGR, and converts in to a 1-channel image and saves it into frameInGray.

 The cvtColor function works with lots of image types. See the OpenCV documentation for more details here http://docs.opencv.org.

Binary

The binarization process compares each pixel with a cut-off value and, if the pixel value is greater than the threshold value, it is assigned as 1. Pixels with a value smaller than the cut-off value are assigned as 0s. This is illustrated in the following code snippet:

```
cvtColor(frameIn, frameInGray, CV_BGR2GRAY);
threshold(frameInGray, frameInBinary, threshold_value,
max_BINARY_value,threshold_type );
```

In the process of converting an image to binary, we need to convert the BGR image to grayscale with the `cvtColor` function to decrease the channel size from 3 to 1. Secondly, we take the grayscale frame and put it into the `threshold` function for binarization. The `Threshold` function saves the new image into a destination frame. This technique is illustrated in this picture:

The threshold change determines which pixels are black or white. The middle image has a smaller threshold whereas the image on the right has a bigger threshold.

Constant thresholding

This operation applies fixed level thresholding to a single-channel array. In general, it is used to get a binary image from a grayscale image. The following code illustrates this:

```
threshold(frameInGray, frameInBinary, threshold_value,
max_BINARY_value,threshold_type );
```

You get the following picture after the operation completes:

For more information please consult the following online documentation:
`http://docs.opencv.org/modules/imgproc/doc/`
`miscellaneous_transformations.html?highlight=threshold`
`#threshold`

Adaptive thresholding

While a conventional thresholding operator uses a global threshold for all pixels, adaptive thresholding changes the threshold locally over the image. Adaptive thresholding is best practice if there is a strong illumination change and shadows. We use this technique as demonstrated in the following code snippet:

```
adaptiveThreshold(frameInGray, frameOut,
MAX_BINARY_VALUE,ADAPTIVE_METHOD, THRESHOLD_TYPE, block_size,
ADAPTIVE_CONSTANT);
```

The operation will result in the following picture:

For more information please visit the following online documentation:
`http://docs.opencv.org/modules/imgproc/doc/`
`miscellaneous_transformations.html#adaptiveThreshold`

Morphological filters

Let's talk about morphological image processing, which is related to the shape of the in an image. Morphological operations are according to a pixel's relative order among its neighbors.

Morphological filters are used to modify structures in binary images. Morphological operators modify the shape of pixel groups instead of their amplitude or value.

Morphological reconstructions are based on recurring uses of dilation or erosion until a marker point is moved. We can perform object boundary detection, hole filling, and region flooding.

The most common morphological operations are erosion and dilation. **Dilation** adds pixels to the boundaries of objects in an image. **Erosion** removes pixels on the object boundaries. **Kernel size** assigns the amount of pixels that are added or subtracted from the objects during the process.

Combinations of dilation and erosion are often used to implement different kinds of morphological processing operations. For instance, the definition of the opening of an image is erosion followed by dilation. Similarly, applying a closing operation to an image is a dilation followed by erosion.

Erosion and dilation

Images with basic morphological manipulations can give very clear information when compared to raw images. Further detection and recognition is dependent on the process that is applied to the image. Let's look closer at the OpenCV usage of both erosion and dilation.

Erosion

We use the `erode` function to apply the erosion operation. The following code snippet is a typical example:

```
erode( frameInBinary, frameOut, kernel );
```

> For more information you can visit the documentation page of erosion filtering at: `http://docs.opencv.org/modules/imgproc/doc/filtering.html?highlight=erode#erode`.

The following picture demonstrates this function's effects:

The preceding series of images show the increasing effect of erosion with respect to kernel size. We see that areas with a white color are overwhelmed by black regions.

Dilation

Dilation tends to highlight white areas, unlike erosion. This function is used as shown here:

```
dilate( frameInBinary,  frameOut , kernel );
```

The following picture demonstrates this function's effects:

 For detailed usage options please visit the following online documentation at http://docs.opencv.org/modules/imgproc/doc/filtering.html?highlight=dilate#dilate.

Opening and closing

Opening and closing operations are combinations of erosion and dilation. Closing operations tend to enlarge white areas in the image. Opening, as opposed to closing, tends to fill white regions.

Closing

Closing operations increase the white areas in the image. Hence, they remove small holes in the image. This line of code demonstrates its usage, using the `morphology` function:

```
morphology(frameInBinary,frameOut,MORPH_CLOSE,kernel);
```

The `morphology` function results in the effects shown in this picture:

Opening

The opening operation removes small objects by enlarging the black areas in the image. White regions are overwhelmed by the bigger black regions. The usage is as follows:

```
morphology(frameInBinary,frameOut,MORPH_OPEN,kernel);
```

The functions show the effects visible in this picture:

 For more information you can visit the documentation page here:
http://docs.opencv.org/modules/imgproc/doc/filtering.
html?highlight=morphologyex#morphologyex

Gradients and edge detection

We will talk about edge detectors in this section. We will look at the following edge detection algorithms: Canny, **Laplacian of Gaussian (LoG)**, and Sobel. We will discuss each of these operators in detail in this section and give OpenCV examples to observe the effects of these operators on an image.

Edge detection is very important in image processing as were the methods we covered earlier in this chapter. By finding edges, lines, and corners we are able to make reasoning to the foreground and background of the image we are processing. After finding and enhancing the boundaries of an image, we can apply detection and recognition algorithms, as we will see in the next few chapters.

The Canny edge detector

Let's introduce you to an important edge detector. The Canny edge detector is a layered method to detect a wide range of edges in an image

John F. Canny developed the Canny edge detector in 1968. The Canny algorithm aims to satisfy three main criteria:

1. **Low error rate**: Detection of edges which are true edges.
2. **Localization**: The distance between edge pixels must be minimized.
3. **Minimal response**: Only one detector response per edge.

The application of the Canny edge detector follows several preordained steps, and they are as follows:

1. Filter out any noise.
2. Find the intensity gradient of the image by applying derivative filters.
3. Find the gradient direction and magnitude.
4. Remove pixels that are not considered edges (a pixel is considered part of an edge if there is a sharp change in gradient).
5. Double thresholding.

It would be nice to look at the code snippet given for the `Canny` operation. As with other operations, we apply blurring and color conversion before applying feature extraction. This can help reduce the noise in the image and improve the results of the `Canny` filter. The `Canny` operation is demonstrated as follows:

```
GaussianBlur( frameIn, frameIn, Size(3,3), 0, 0, BORDER_DEFAULT );
cvtColor( frameIn, frameInGray, CV_RGB2GRAY );
Canny( frameInGray, frameOut, canny_low_threshold,
canny_low_threshold*CANNY_RATIO, CANNY_KERNEL_SIZE );
```

This operation results in the following picture:

In the preceding series of images, we see Canny edge detection with the changing values of the minimum threshold. By changing the minimum threshold, we change the response of the Canny edge detector. Note that the chapter project given at the end of this chapter will help you to experience the effect of changing filter arguments. For now, it is better to first understand how this filter works.

We smooth the image for noise spikes and then apply a conversion from BGR space to grayscale, as shown in the following code snippet:

```
GaussianBlur( frameIn, frameIn, Size(3,3), 0, 0, BORDER_DEFAULT );
cvtColor( frameIn, frameInGray, CV_RGB2GRAY );
```

Let's check the Canny function, as shown in the following code snippet. The Canny operation uses two thresholds and their ratio must be around 1:2 to 1:3. As you may guess, this function also uses a kernel and we pass the kernel size to the function. Again, it is nice to recall that a bigger kernel size has a bigger impact on images:

```
Canny( frameInGray, frameOut, canny_low_threshold,
canny_low_threshold*CANNY_RATIO, CANNY_KERNEL_SIZE );
```

Laplacian of Gaussian filter

The Laplacian is a second derivative operator which highlights regions of rapid intensity change. For this reason Laplacian is often used for edge detection. The Laplacian is applied to an image that has first been smoothed with something approximated to a Gaussian smoothing filter in order to reduce its sensitivity to noise. This operation normally takes a single gray level image as input and produces another gray level image as output. For this operation we need to design a kernel that will mimic Gaussian distribution. Since the input is represented as a set of discrete pixels, we have to find a discrete convolution kernel that can approximate the second derivatives in the definition of the Laplacian. Two commonly used kernels are shown here, 4-connected and 8-connected grids respectively.

4-connected grid:

0	-1	0
-1	4	-1
0	-1	0

8-connected grid:

-1	-1	-1
-1	8	-1
-1	-1	-1

Now let's go through the example code:

```
GaussianBlur( frameIn, frameIn, Size(3,3), 0, 0, BORDER_DEFAULT );
cvtColor( frameIn, frameInGray, CV_RGB2GRAY );
Laplacian( frameInGray, frameOut, LAPLACIAN_DEPTH, KERNEL_SIZE,
LAPLACIAN_SCALE, LAPLACIAN_DELTA, BORDER_DEFAULT );
```

The code results in the following effect on the picture:

Laplacian of Gaussian is particularly good at highlighting drastic changes such as white numbers on a black jersey. It is designed to find not ordinary edges but drastic ones.

Let's apply a Gaussian blur in order to reduce noise. Note that we override the blurred image on the source image. We do this because we will no longer use the source image:

```
GaussianBlur( frameIn, frameIn, Size(3,3), 0, 0, BORDER_DEFAULT );
```

Convert the image to grayscale:

```
cvtColor( frameIn, frameInGray, CV_RGB2GRAY );
```

Apply the Laplacian operator to the blurred and gray-scaled image. As we see in the preceding image, LoG finds intensity jumps, as shown in this code snippet

```
Laplacian( frameInGray, frameOut, LAPLACIAN_DEPTH, KERNEL_SIZE,
LAPLACIAN_SCALE, LAPLACIAN_DELTA, BORDER_DEFAULT );
```

Sobel

The Sobel filter or Sobel operator is frequently used for edge detection. There are two 3 x 3 mask matrices that convolve with the image data. Sobel is a popular preprocessing stage operation.

The two Sobel operators find lines—vertical and horizontal.

Vertical Sobel filter:

1	2	1
0	0	0
-1	-2	-1

Horizontal Sobel filter:

1	0	-1
2	0	-2
1	0	-1

Let's look closer the following code for a `Sobel` operation. As usual, smoothing and color conversion are applied before the `Sobel` filter. Then, the `Sobel` filter is applied to the grayscale image of the original image to get the output image:

```
GaussianBlur( frameIn, frameIn, Size(3,3), 0, 0, BORDER_DEFAULT );
cvtColor( frameIn, frameInGray, CV_RGB2GRAY );
Sobel( frameInGray, frameOut, SOBEL_DEPTH, SOBEL_X_DERIVATIVE,
SOBEL_Y_DERIVATIVE, 2*sobel_kernel_size+1, SOBEL_SCALE,
SOBEL_DELTA, BORDER_DEFAULT );
```

The code results in these effects:

Get rid of the noise by applying the Gaussian blurring operation:

```
GaussianBlur( frameIn, frameIn, Size(3,3), 0, 0, BORDER_DEFAULT );
```

For the sake of edge detection we convert our image to gray-level:

```
cvtColor( frameIn, frameInGray, CV_RGB2GRAY );
```

The `Sobel` function takes the degree of derivatives of both x and y directions, SOBEL_DEPTH, SOBEL_X_DERIVATIVE, SOBEL_Y_DERIVATIVE respectively, as shown in the following code. Other than those derivative order arguments, a scaling, an offset value and border extrapolation arguments are given:

```
Sobel( frameInGray, frameOut, SOBEL_DEPTH, SOBEL_X_DERIVATIVE,
       SOBEL_Y_DERIVATIVE, 2*sobel_kernel_size+1, SOBEL_SCALE,
       SOBEL_DELTA, BORDER_DEFAULT );
```

 For more detail please visit the `Sobel` filter documentation page at http://docs.opencv.org/modules/imgproc/doc/filtering.html?highlight=sobel#sobel.

Custom filtering

The OpenCV function `filter2D` gives the user the ability to design custom kernels. Sometimes it is best to design a kernel for a particular process.

The following code implements a smoothing operation to the source image with an increasing effect.

Let's go through an OpenCV example from http://docs.opencv.org/doc/tutorials/imgproc/imgtrans/filter_2d/filter_2d.html:

```cpp
#include "opencv2/imgproc/imgproc.hpp"
#include "opencv2/highgui/highgui.hpp"
#include <stdlib.h>
#include <stdio.h>

using namespace cv;

/** @function main */
int main ( int argc, char** argv )
{
 /// Declare variables
  Mat src, dst;

  Mat kernel;
  Point anchor;
  double delta;
  int ddepth;
  int kernel_size;
  char window_name[] = "filter2D Demo";

  int c;

 /// Load an image
  src - imread( argv[1] );

  if( !src.data )
  { return -1; }

 /// Create window
  namedWindow( window_name, CV_WINDOW_AUTOSIZE );

 /// Initialize arguments for the filter
  anchor = Point( -1, -1 );
  delta = 0;
  ddepth = -1;
```

```
/// Loop - Will filter the image with different kernel sizes each
0.5 seconds
  int ind = 0;
  while( true )
    {
      c = waitKey(500);
  /// Press 'ESC' to exit the program
      if( (char)c == 27 )
        { break; }

  /// Update kernel size for a normalized box filter
      kernel_size = 3 + 2*( ind%5 );
      kernel = Mat::ones( kernel_size, kernel_size, CV_32F )/
(float)(kernel_size*kernel_size);

  /// Apply filter
      filter2D(src, dst, ddepth , kernel, anchor, delta,
BORDER_DEFAULT );
      imshow( window_name, dst );
      ind++;
    }

  return 0;
}
```

The following effects are visible in this picture:

As we stated earlier, the kernel size increases by a factor of two. As a result, the smoothing operation effect increases. We can see the original, mild and heavily filtered image.

Initialize the arguments for the linear filter. In this context the anchor object represents the pivot point of the kernel:

```
anchor = Point( -1, -1 );
delta = 0;
ddepth = -1;
```

We define the kernel for the filter:

```
kernel_size = 3 + 2*( ind%5 );
kernel = Mat::ones( kernel_size, kernel_size, CV_32F )/
(float)(kernel_size*kernel_size);
```

After setting the kernel, it is necessary to generate the filter itself by using the filter2D OpenCV function.

```
filter2D(src, dst, ddepth , kernel, anchor, delta,
BORDER_DEFAULT );
```

Histogram equalization

The Histogram is a count of the intensity levels in the image. Analysis of the histogram gives useful information about image contrast. Image histograms are important in many areas of image processing, most notably compression, segmentation, and thresholding.

Now we would like to introduce the histogram equalization operation. This operation is a technique for adjusting image intensities to enhance contrast, as demonstrated here:

```
cvtColor( frameIn, frameIn, CV_BGR2GRAY );
equalizeHist( frameIn, frameOut );
```

The `equalizeHist` function brings about the following effects in the picture:

The equalized image on the right is more vivid and the colors are brighter. We can differentiate objects more easily.

Let go through the code. First we convert image in grayscale:

```
cvtColor( frameIn, frameIn, CV_BGR2GRAY );
```

Apply histogram equalization with the function:

```
equalizeHist( frameIn, frameOut );
```

Chapter project

Let's look at the filters we have covered in this chapter. With this comprehensive OpenCV project you will be able to interactively see filtering effects on the given image.

This project covers Canny, Sobel, erosion, dilation and the thresholding operation in individual windows with a trackbar to dynamically change the filter variable which dynamically updates the processed image. Please note that practising is the only way to understand these concepts. After studying this project please make alterations to the code to see changes.

In addition to dynamic manipulation capabilities, we cluster each operation in cannyOperation, sobelOperation, erosionOperation, dilationOperation and thresholdingOperation functions to make the code much more modular and cleaner. Let's go through the code:

```
#include "opencv2/imgproc/imgproc.hpp"
#include "opencv2/highgui/highgui.hpp"
#include <stdlib.h>
#include <stdio.h>

using namespace cv;
/// Definetions
#define MAX_BINARY_VALUE (255)
#define MID_BINARY_VALUE (127)
#define SOBEL_X_DERIVATIVE (1)
#define SOBEL_Y_DERIVATIVE (1)
#define SOBEL_MAX_KERNEL_SIZE (15)
#define SOBEL_DELTA (0)
#define SOBEL_SCALE (1)
#define SOBEL_DEPTH (CV_8U)
#define CANNY_KERNEL_SIZE (3)
#define CANNY_MAX_LOW_THRESHOLD (100)
#define CANNY_RATIO (3)
#define MAX_MORPHOLOGY_KERNEL_SIZE (21)
/// Global Variables

Mat frameIn, frameInGray,frameOut, frameInBinary;

/// Canny Variables
int canny_low_threshold;

/// Sobel Variables
int sobel_kernel_size = 0;

/// Erosion and Dilation Variables
int erosion_kernel = 0, dilation_kernel = 0;

/// Thresholding Variables
int threshold_value = MID_BINARY_VALUE;
```

```
/// Function Prototypes
void cannyOperation(int, void*);
void sobelOperation(int, void*);
void erosionOperation( int, void* );
void dilationOperation( int, void* );
void thresholdingOperation( int, void* );

/// Main Function
int main( int argc, char** argv )
{
    frameIn = imread( argv[1] );

    if( !frameIn.data )
    { return -1; }

    ///Apply Smoothing
    GaussianBlur(frameIn, frameIn, Size(3,3), 0.0);

    /// Convert Source
    cvtColor( frameIn, frameInGray, CV_BGR2GRAY );

    /// Create Windows
    namedWindow( "Canny Operation", CV_WINDOW_AUTOSIZE );
    namedWindow( "Erosion Operation", CV_WINDOW_AUTOSIZE );
    namedWindow( "Dilation Operation", CV_WINDOW_AUTOSIZE );
    namedWindow( "Sobel Operation", CV_WINDOW_AUTOSIZE );
    namedWindow( "Thresholding Operation", CV_WINDOW_AUTOSIZE );

    /// Create Trackbars for Canny, Sobel, Erosion, Dilation, and
Thresholding Operations
    createTrackbar( "Low Threshold:", "Canny Operation",
&canny_low_threshold, CANNY_MAX_LOW_THRESHOLD, cannyOperation );
    createTrackbar( "Kernel size:", "Sobel Operation",
&sobel_kernel_size, SOBEL_MAX_KERNEL_SIZE, sobelOperation );
    createTrackbar( "Kernel size:", "Erosion Operation",
&erosion_kernel, MAX_MORPHOLOGY_KERNEL_SIZE, erosionOperation );
    createTrackbar( "Kernel size:", "Dilation
Operation",&dilation_kernel,
MAX_MORPHOLOGY_KERNEL_SIZE,dilationOperation );
    createTrackbar( "Threshold Value", "Thresholding Operation",
&threshold_value, MAX_BINARY_VALUE, thresholdingOperation );

    /// Call Filter Functions
    cannyOperation(0, 0);
    sobelOperation(0,0);
```

```
    dilationOperation(0, 0);
    erosionOperation(0, 0);
    thresholdingOperation(0, 0);

    /// Wait until user exit program by pressing a key
    waitKey(0);

    return 0;
}
/**
 * @function cannyOperation
 *
 */
void cannyOperation(int, void*)
{
    /// Canny detector
    Canny( frameInGray, frameOut, canny_low_threshold,
canny_low_threshold*CANNY_RATIO, CANNY_KERNEL_SIZE );
    imshow( "Canny Operation", frameOut );
}
/**
 * @function sobelOperation
 *
 */
void sobelOperation(int, void*)
{
    ///Sobel
    Sobel( frameInGray, frameOut, SOBEL_DEPTH, SOBEL_X_DERIVATIVE,
SOBEL_Y_DERIVATIVE, 2*sobel_kernel_size+1, SOBEL_SCALE,
SOBEL_DELTA, BORDER_DEFAULT );
    imshow( "Sobel Operation", frameOut );
}


/**
 * @function erosionOperation
 *
 */
void erosionOperation( int, void* )
{
    threshold( frameInGray, frameInBinary, MID_BINARY_VALUE,
MAX_BINARY_VALUE, THRESH_BINARY);
    Mat element = getStructuringElement( MORPH_RECT,
                                         Size( 2*erosion_kernel +
1, 2*erosion_kernel+1 ),
```

```
                                                    Point( erosion_kernel,
    erosion_kernel ) );

        /// Apply the erosion operation
        erode( frameInBinary, frameOut, element );
        imshow( "Erosion Operation", frameOut );
    }


    /**
     * @function dilationOperation
     *
     */
    void dilationOperation( int, void* )
    {
        threshold( frameInGray, frameInBinary, MID_BINARY_VALUE,
    MAX_BINARY_VALUE,THRESH_BINARY);
        Mat element = getStructuringElement( MORPH_RECT,
                                            Size( 2*dilation_kernel +
    1, 2*dilation_kernel+1 ),
                                            Point( dilation_kernel,
    dilation_kernel ) );
        /// Apply the dilation operation
        dilate( frameInBinary, frameOut, element );
        imshow( "Dilation Operation", frameOut );
    }
    /**
     * @function thresholdingOperation
     *
     */
    void thresholdingOperation( int, void* )
    {
        threshold( frameInGray, frameOut, threshold_value,
    MAX_BINARY_VALUE,THRESH_BINARY );
        imshow( "Thresholding Operation", frameOut );
    }
```

From top to bottom in the project, definitions are declared first. Then, dynamically changing variables of trackbars are declared which store changed trackbar values. Function declarations are followed by the main function. Now, time to look into the main function:

```
    int main( int argc, char** argv )
    {
        frameIn = imread( argv[1] );
```

```
    if( !frameIn.data )
    { return -1; }

    ///Apply Smoothing
    GaussianBlur(frameIn, frameIn, Size(3,3), 0.0);

    /// Convert Source
    cvtColor( frameIn, frameInGray, CV_BGR2GRAY );

    /// Create Windows
    namedWindow( "Canny Operation", CV_WINDOW_AUTOSIZE );
    namedWindow( "Erosion Operation", CV_WINDOW_AUTOSIZE );
    namedWindow( "Dilation Operation", CV_WINDOW_AUTOSIZE );
    namedWindow( "Sobel Operation", CV_WINDOW_AUTOSIZE );
    namedWindow( "Thresholding Operation", CV_WINDOW_AUTOSIZE );

    /// Create Trackbars for Canny, Sobel, Erosion, Dilation, and
Thresholding Operations
    createTrackbar( "Low Threshold:", "Canny Operation",
&canny_low_threshold, CANNY_MAX_LOW_THRESHOLD, cannyOperation );
    createTrackbar( "Kernel size:", "Sobel Operation",
&sobel_kernel_size, SOBEL_MAX_KERNEL_SIZE, sobelOperation );
    createTrackbar( "Kernel size:", "Erosion Operation",
&erosion_kernel, MAX_MORPHOLOGY_KERNEL_SIZE, erosionOperation );
    createTrackbar( "Kernel size:", "Dilation
Operation",&dilation_kernel,
MAX_MORPHOLOGY_KERNEL_SIZE,dilationOperation );
    createTrackbar( "Threshold Value", "Thresholding Operation",
&threshold_value, MAX_BINARY_VALUE, thresholdingOperation );

    /// Call Filter Functions
    cannyOperation(0, 0);
    sobelOperation(0,0);
    dilationOperation(0, 0);
    erosionOperation(0, 0);
    thresholdingOperation(0, 0);

    /// Wait until user exit program by pressing a key
    waitKey(0);

    return 0;
}
```

Firstly, we load the source image and check if it is properly loaded. Since we want to perform smoothing before each of the filters, we apply this operation once and rewrite the original image. After the smoothing step, we convert our image to grayscale in order to prepare the right type of image for the filtering operations.

We created our windows and their trackbars for every filtering operation and we give a text to print, a window name to bind, a variable to store trackbar changes, a maximum value for the trackbar and the corresponding function to execute with the updated trackbar value to execute respectively. Lastly we initiated our filtering operation functions. Let's look at the `cannyOperation` function:

```
void cannyOperation(int, void*)
{
    Canny( frameInGray, frameOut, canny_low_threshold,
canny_low_threshold*CANNY_RATIO, CANNY_KERNEL_SIZE );
    imshow( "Canny Operation", frameOut );
}
```

The `cannyOperation` function is called when the trackbar in the Canny operation window is moved. The function runs with the updated variable, `canny_low_threshold` and the newly processed image is displayed in the same window. In this function we call the OpenCV `Canny` function to perform the operation. Let's look at the `sobelOperation` function:

```
void sobelOperation(int, void*)
{
    Sobel( frameInGray, frameOut, SOBEL_DEPTH, SOBEL_X_DERIVATIVE,
SOBEL_Y_DERIVATIVE, 2*sobel_kernel_size+1, SOBEL_SCALE,
SOBEL_DELTA, BORDER_DEFAULT );
    imshow( "Sobel Operation", frameOut );

}
```

The `sobelOperation` function calls the OpenCV `Sobel` function. Let's examine two of the parameters of the function. `SOBEL_X_DERIVATIVE` and `SOBEL_Y_DERIVATIVE` indicate the order of the derivative of the kernel in both x and y directions. These are set to 1 for each of them. After the filtering operation, the newly processed image is shown in the Sobel operation window:

```
void erosionOperation( int, void* )
{
  threshold( frameInGray, frameInBinary, MID_BINARY_VALUE, MAX_BINARY_
VALUE, THRESH_BINARY);
```

```
    Mat element = getStructuringElement( MORPH_RECT, Size( 2*erosion_
kernel + 1, 2*erosion_kernel+1 ),
Point( erosion_kernel, erosion_kernel ) );
    // Apply the erosion operation
    erode( frameInBinary, frameOut, element );
    imshow( "Erosion Operation", frameOut );
}
```

For the erosion process we first convert `frameInGray` into the binary form. Then, we construct the kernel according to the trackbar change. After that, we call the `erode` function to update the image with the structuring element which is shaped like a rectangle. We give the shape of the kernel by giving the first parameter of the `getStructuringElement` function as the `MORPH_RECT` definition. The newly processed image is displayed with the `imshow` function as usual. Let's see the `dilationOperation` function:

```
void dilationOperation( int, void* )
{
    threshold( frameInGray, frameInBinary, MID_BINARY_VALUE, MAX_BINARY_
VALUE, THRESH_BINARY);
    Mat element = getStructuringElement( MORPH_RECT, Size( 2*dilation_
kernel +1, 2*dilation_kernel+1 ), Point( dilation_kernel, dilation_
kernel ) );
    dilate( frameInBinary, frameOut, element );
    imshow( "Dilation Operation", frameOut );
}
```

There is a very similar operation with `dilationOperation`. As in erosion, we construct the structuring element with the `getStructuringElement` function and apply dilation with the `dilate` function. Let's look at the `thresholdingOperation` function:

```
void thresholdingOperation( int, void* )
{
    threshold( frameInGray, frameOut, threshold_value,
MAX_BINARY_VALUE, THRESH_BINARY );
    imshow( "Thresholding Operation", frameOut );
}
```

The `thresholdingOperation` function is called when the trackbar in the thresholding window is moved. The OpenCV threshold function performs the thresholding operation. We use the binary threshold method as we pass the corresponding parameter as `THRESH_BINARY`. A new image is represented by the `imshow` function in the corresponding window.

Summary

In this chapter you have learned about the filtering mechanisms of OpenCV. You learned the most common filtering techniques and how to use them properly. In the chapter project, we have implemented a comprehensive filtering application in which you can see the effects of different filters.

After filtering the vision data properly you are now ready for processing! Get ready for the next chapter! The next chapter gives a description of image data processing, which is typically a small set of data.

5
Processing Vision Data with OpenCV

In this chapter, you will learn about extracting meaningful features from images or videos by applying processing techniques to the data. You will find the approaches which are used to extract small pieces of meaningful information from a huge amount of image data. At the end, you'll use these meaningful features for basic detection purposes. This chapter will give you a wide perspective view on extracting features from vision data (such as an image or a video) and the relevant OpenCV structures will also be explained.

Extracting features

Vision data itself is a multidimensional pixel array and, when we see this type of data, our brain intuitively extracts information from it. Actually, extracting such high level information from a dataset is a very complex operation. This operation should take a huge amount of zeros and ones as the input data and it should convert this data into a conclusion such as, "Yes, this is a car!", or sometimes even, "This is Randy's car!". Maybe this process sounds very easy for you but, for computers, it is not.

A computer and the human brain work very differently. As a result, a computer is much more powerful when making calculations and the brain is much more capable with high level tasks such as scene interpretation. So, this chapter concentrates on a weak element of computer science. Despite this, it is surely possible to interpret vision scenes intelligently by using computers, but the approach of extracting meaningful information from vision data is an indirect way of approaching the job. Learning this indirect approach is integral to understanding the intelligent part of computer vision science.

Since vision data is composed of digital data consisting of a huge amount of numbers and raw computer power is used in calculations, the solution is to extract a more descriptive, small set of numbers from the image, and this is called the feature extraction process.

OpenCV has a lot of support for feature extraction methods, from simple operations to complex ones. Even with sophisticated algorithms, it is really simple to use. In this chapter, we'll look at the most important feature extraction mechanisms and give tips on the process. The feature extraction phase of the computer vision process is very important because detection and recognition rely on the information which is gathered by feature extraction.

Using basic statistics

Imagine a basic vision problem for a simple scene—detecting the existence of any object on a table. The vision system has to decide if the table surface is empty or not. It should be really easy to solve the problem by using the basic statistics of the image. The following screenshot shows an empty table on the left and a table with different things on top of it on the right:

Now, let's build a computer vision system which can detect objects on the table. As you can see, the table surface has a pattern which we don't want to deal with. By smoothing the image, this detail can be removed. We should then convert the image to binary and most of the objects will look white, while the table surface is black. But a problem could arise with the color of the wallet. As you can see from the picture on the right, the wallet is more or less the same color as the table surface. Even so, we should use the edge image because the edge detector can find the edges of the wallet. We can add a thresholded image to the edge image to get more detailed input.

All of these techniques were discussed in the previous chapter, so you already have all the knowledge necessary to do this. The empty table in this image will appear fully black and, for any object on the table, the binary image will include white areas. By calculating the mean of the image, we should be able to ascertain if there is an object on the table or not!

Let's code this algorithm and then see the results. Here is the code you will find inside the `tabletop_object_detector.cpp` file:

```cpp
#include <opencv2/core/core.hpp>
#include "opencv2/imgproc/imgproc.hpp"
#include <opencv2/highgui/highgui.hpp>
#include <iostream>

using namespace cv;
using namespace std;

#define MAX_KERNEL_LENGTH  (19)
#define MEAN_THRESH_VAL (1)

int main( int argc, char** argv )
{
 if(argc != 2)
 {
 cout << "Missing argument"<< endl; return -1;
 }

 Mat org_image, blurred_image,binary_image,edge_image;
 org_image = imread(argv[1], CV_LOAD_IMAGE_GRAYSCALE);

 if(org_image.data==NULL)
 {
 cout << "Empty image"<< endl; return -1;
 }

 for (int i = 1; i < MAX_KERNEL_LENGTH; i = i + 2 )
 {
    GaussianBlur( org_image, blurred_image, Size(i,i),0,0);
 }

 threshold(org_image,binary_image,170,255,THRESH_BINARY);

 Canny(blurred_image, edge_image,18,36);
```

```
binary_image += edge_image;

Scalar mean_scalar, stddev_scalar;
meanStdDev(binary_image,mean_scalar,stddev_scalar);
double mean_value, stddev_value;
mean_value = mean_scalar.val[0];
stddev_value = stddev_scalar.val[0];

cout << "mean: "<< mean_value << endl <<"stddev: "<< stddev_value <<
endl;

if(mean_value > MEAN_THRESH_VAL)
    cout << "Table is not empty!" << endl;
else
    cout << "Table is empty!" << endl;

imwrite("binary_image.png",binary_image);
return 0;
}
```

Before looking at the additions to the table-top object detector code, let's look at the binary output images for the empty table and the table with objects. You should call the application executable with the table images as described in *Chapter 2, Fundamentals and Installation of OpenCV*. The following screenshot shows two images, an empty table on the left and a table with various objects on top of it on the right:

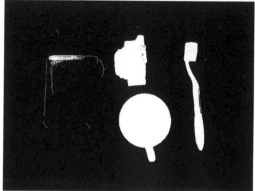

You can see that we have got what we expected! The console output for the empty table is:

```
mean: 0
stddev: 0
Table is empty!
```

And console output for the table with different objects is:

```
mean: 24.2457
stddev: 74.7984
Table is not empty!
```

As you can see, we represented the whole scene image with two double numbers—mean, and standard deviation. It is possible to develop a table-top object existence detector just by using the mean information. Here the mean value which we used is the extracted feature from the image and it is possible to describe the high-level existence information by using this feature instead of the whole image data. Now, let's examine the following code:

```
for (int i = 1; i < MAX_KERNEL_LENGTH; i = i + 2 )
  {
  GaussianBlur( org_image, blurred_image, Size( i, i ), 0, 0 );
  }
```

Firstly, the image is loaded as grayscale, so further grayscale conversion is not needed. We then blur the image to remove the pattern of the table.

After blurring the image, we should get the thresholded image and the edge image. For thresholding, a constant threshold is used to get rid of small details. We obtain the threshold value 170 empirically and you can experiment with other values to see how this affects the process. The following are the typical threshold function arguments:

```
threshold(org_image,binary_image,170,255,THRESH_BINARY);
```

And similarly, edge image is calculated by using the Canny algorithm:

```
Canny(blurred_image, edge_image,18,36);
```

The edge image is then added to the binary image. The purpose of this operation is to retain both the edge information and the object area information. In this way it is possible to detect even challenging objects, such as those which are the same color as the table itself. Combining two binarization approaches boosts the success rate of the algorithm. Adding one image to another means adding the value of each pixel together from both images. The resulting image is saved as a binary image which overwrites what was previously saved as the binary image, as shown in this line of code:

```
binary_image += edge_image;
```

After getting the binary image with edges, the feature extraction phase follows. The mean value and standard deviation statistics of the image are calculated as follows:

```
Scalar mean_scalar, stddev_scalar;
 meanStdDev(binary_image,mean_scalar,stddev_scalar);
 double mean_value, stddev_value;
 mean_value = mean_scalar.val[0];
 stddev_value = stddev_scalar.val[0];
```

The next step is the decision phase. As you can see from the console outputs, both the mean value and the standard deviation value can be used to decide the object existence status on the table surface. We used the mean value, as follows:

```
if(mean_value > MEAN_THRESH_VAL)
  cout << "Table is not empty!" << endl;
 else
  cout << "Table is empty!" << endl;
```

Mean threshold values are also calculated empirically. Since an empty table produces a zero mean value, a mean value greater than one will work. Actually, a mean value which is greater than zero will also work but here we have left a margin of error of one. If the table image wasn't perfectly illuminated (let's say there was some reflection or a scratch on the table), this mean threshold value could be raised to leave a larger margin.

As you can see, with a few simple steps we have built an object existence detector. But, for some problems, it is not sufficient to use such features and statistics to reach a conclusion. Even for complex operations, OpenCV provides many processing interfaces. Because there are so many, we'll mention the most important ones and you can consult the OpenCV documentation to find examples. Once you learn which method is used for which purpose, you can easily integrate these methods into your application.

Using color features

Color information is sometimes a distinctive property between objects and scenes. In such cases, utilizing this property aids success. The most difficult part of using the color property is that it varies greatly with illumination changes when we use RGB values. To suppress illumination effects, the HSV color space can be used. The value term stands for the intensity (or brightness) and the hue term gives information on color features. Hue is not affected by big changes in lighting, so it can be used to identify information from different parts of a scene with different lighting conditions. To be able to convert a BGR image to HSV space, the following function can be used:

```
cvtColor(org_image, hsv_image, COLOR_BGR2HSV);
```

After converting the image space to HSV, it is possible to check if the target pixels are in a specified range by using the following function. To check the red objects for example, the following code snippet can be used:

```
inRange(hsv_image, Scalar(0, 0, 0), Scalar(175, 255, 255),
hsv_thresholded_image);
```

The inRange function filters the input image in a given low and high range and writes the resulting image to its latest parameter. By calculating the basic statistics of the resulting hsv_thresholded_image, you can then see if there is a red object. This usage is the basis of color processing techniques. You'll find the usage example of these functions in the last chapter!

Using template matching features

If you are searching for a specific shape or template, comparing the template with relevant image regions or comparing two images directly are both good ideas. A cross correlation operation can be used to investigate the similarities between image matrices. OpenCV also has a template matching function called matchTemplate in its object detection libraries. This function matchTemplate takes the following arguments:

```
void ocl::matchTemplate(const oclMat& image, const oclMat& templ,
oclMat& result, int method)
```

 For more information on the template matching function, and more, please consult the OpenCV documentation found at http://docs. opencv.org/modules/ocl/doc/object_detection.html.

Using contours

When you are trying to get information about the shape of an object, seeing the contours of the object will help a lot. Contours of objects can be used as features to make structural shape analysis. OpenCV has a contour finder function which can be applied to binary images.

```
void findContours(InputOutputArray image, OutputArrayOfArrays
contours, int mode, int method, Point offset=Point())
```

It makes sense to apply the findContours function over an edge image if you are investigating the contours of a shape. So, it can be applied after a Canny operation. As the next step shows, it would be good to draw the found contours. OpenCV has a function called as drawContours to draw contours:

```
void drawContours(InputOutputArray image, InputArrayOfArrays
contours, int contourIdx, const Scalar& color, int thickness=1,
int lineType=8, InputArray hierarchy=noArray(), int
maxLevel=INT_MAX, Point offset=Point() )
```

A sample code snippet for these two functions is shown here:

```
Mat canny_output;
vector<vector<Point> > contours;
vector<Vec4i> hierarchy;
int thresh = 100, max_thresh = 255;
RNG rng(12345);
/// Detect edges using canny
Canny( gray_image, canny_output, thresh, thresh*2, 3 );
/// Find contours
findContours( canny_output, contours, hierarchy, CV_RETR_TREE,
CV_CHAIN_APPROX_SIMPLE, Point(0, 0) );
/// Draw contours
Mat drawing = Mat::zeros( canny_output.size(), CV_8UC3 );
for( int i = 0; i< contours.size(); i++ )
{
    Scalar color = Scalar( rng.uniform(0, 255),
rng.uniform(0,255), rng.uniform(0,255) );
    drawContours( drawing, contours, i, color, 2, 8, hierarchy, 0,
Point() );
}
```

Here you can see the output of the code. The contours of the owl are detected and drawn with random colors:

Using the convex hull

Object shape is generally a bounded subset of the plane and the convex hull can be considered as the shape formed by a stretched layer of band around the object shape.

The convex hull is a very important shape descriptor for contours. The convex hull helps to distinguish between objects and object states, especially for shapes with a skeleton. Hand gesture application illustrates the benefits of the convex hull. In the following picture, you can see hand gestures and contours in blue, and the relevant convex hulls in red:

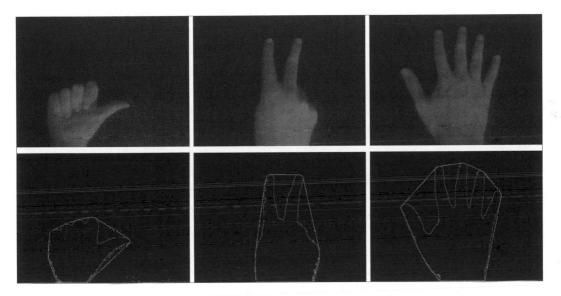

As you can see, convex hull lines are different with each hand gesture. By using line numbers and angles between lines it is possible to detect or recognize hand gestures. The convex hull is a good feature extraction algorithm to do this. The code snippet is as follows:

```
Mat src_copy = src.clone();
Mat threshold_output;
vector<vector<Point> > contours;
vector<Vec4i> hierarchy;
imwrite("hull_org.png",src_copy);

threshold( src_gray, threshold_output, thresh, 255,
THRESH_BINARY );
/// Find contours
```

```
    findContours( threshold_output, contours, hierarchy, RETR_TREE,
CHAIN_APPROX_SIMPLE, Point(0, 0) );

    /// Find the convex hull object for each contour
    vector<vector<Point> >hull( contours.size() );
    for( size_t i = 0; i < contours.size(); i++ )
    {
      convexHull( Mat(contours[i]), hull[i]);
    }

    /// Draw contours + hull results
    Mat drawing = Mat::zeros( threshold_output.size(), CV_8UC3 );
    for( size_t i = 0; i< contours.size(); i++ )
    {
        Scalar color = Scalar( rng.uniform(0, 255),
rng.uniform(0,255), rng.uniform(0,255) );
        drawContours( drawing, contours, (int)i, Scalar(255,0,0),
2, 8, vector<Vec4i>(), 0, Point() );
        drawContours( drawing, hull, (int)i, Scalar(0,0,255), 2, 8,
vector<Vec4i>(), 0, Point() );
    }
```

The difference to the contour example is the convexHull function itself. The convexHull function takes contours as input and calculates hulls. A prototype of the function is shown here:

```
void convexHull(InputArray points, OutputArray hull, bool
clockwise=false, bool returnPoints=true )
```

Another important feature of the convex hull is in finding defects. Any deviation of the object shape from the convex hulls can be considered as a convexity defect. Defects are also used as features. The function prototype is shown here:

```
void convexityDefects(InputArray contour, InputArray convexhull,
OutputArray convexityDefects)
```

Using moments

Image moments are useful features in the detection or recognition process. If you need information on the area or centre of gravity of objects, moments will help you a lot. An image moment is a certain particular weighted average of the image pixels' intensities, or a function of such moments, usually chosen to have some attractive property or interpretation. These features are widely used in segmentation.

OpenCV supports the calculation of moments with two functions, shown here:

```
Moments moments(InputArray array, bool binaryImage=false )
void HuMoments(const Moments& moments, double hu[7])
```

The `HuMoments` function is invariant from lots of operations, such as rotation. Benefiting from these interfaces will improve your segmentation algorithm, so it is good to be familiar with these useful features.

 For more information and an example application please visit `http://dalab.se.sjtu.edu.cn/docs/opencv/docs.opencv.org/2.4/doc/tutorials/imgproc/shapedescriptors/moments/moments.html`.

Using the Hough transform

The Hough transform is a useful feature extraction technique used in computer vision. The basic aim of the technique is to extract defected or perfect instances of an object shape by voting to an accumulator. It is possible to detect lines and shapes (which might be basic, or complex) by using the Hough transform. It is often used to detect lines, curves, and circles in computer vision applications. The important part, the efficiency of the Hough transform, depends on the clarity and quality of the input data. So, applying the Hough transform after a good edge detection procedure improves the efficiency of the algorithm. Normally, generic implementation of the Hough transform is classified as a slow algorithm because of its heavy computation load, but the probabilistic implementation of the Hough transform mostly eliminates this con by providing lots of pros.

The Hough transform is also used in the segmentation process. When the scene consists of a combination of lines, Hough line detection-based segmentation helps a lot. An example is bookshelf segmentation, as shown in the following picture:

OpenCV has three Hough transform implementations, two of them are for lines and one of them is for circles. Here, in the following code, you can see the functions for the standard Hough transform for lines, the probabilistic Hough transform for lines, and the Hough transform for circles, respectively. The probabilistic transform (HoughLinesP) works faster than the normal one (HoughLines).

```
void HoughLines(InputArray image, OutputArray lines, double rho,
double theta, int threshold, double srn=0, double stn=0 )
void HoughLinesP(InputArray image, OutputArray lines, double rho,
double theta, int threshold, double minLineLength=0, double
maxLineGap=0 )
void HoughCircles(InputArray image, OutputArray circles, int
method, double dp, double minDist, double param1=100, double
param2=100, int minRadius=0, int maxRadius=0 )
```

Using corners

In some applications, it is necessary to find matching points between frames and establish temporal connections between these corner points. This is important if we have multiple images and we know that they are related to each other because we can extract much more information from this set of images. Corner detection is frequently used in object tracking applications.

OpenCV has a rich set of interfaces for corner detection. One of the best is the Harris corner detection technique. The Harris corner detection technique is a rotation invariant corner detection technique. The interface of the Harris corner detector in OpenCV is as follows:

```
void cornerHarris(InputArray src, OutputArray dst, int
blockSize, int ksize, double k, int borderType=BORDER_DEFAULT
)
```

For more information and an example application of the Harris corner detector consult the OpenCV documentation, found at http://docs.opencv.org/doc/tutorials/features2d/trackingmotion/harris_detector/harris_detector.html.

There is another OpenCV interface which provides richer opportunities for corner detection and it also supports the Shi-Tomasi corner detector as well as the Harris corner detector. OpenCV has excellent features to track interfaces for corner detection. The interface of the function is as follows:

```
void goodFeaturesToTrack(InputArray image, OutputArray
corners, int maxCorners, double qualityLevel, double
minDistance, InputArray mask=noArray(), int blockSize=3, bool
useHarrisDetector=false, double k=0.04 )
```

For more information and an example application of the goodFeaturesToTrack corner detector, consult the OpenCV documentation found at http://docs.opencv.org/doc/tutorials/features2d/trackingmotion/good_features_to_track/good_features_to_track.html.

Using SIFT

SIFT stands for the **Scale Invariant Feature Transform (SIFT)** algorithm. Harris corner detector is a rotation invariant technique for corner detection, but what about scale? Harris corner detection is a scale variant algorithm. In real cases, significant changes in scale cause the algorithm to fail. In such cases, SIFT helps a lot.

SIFT finds useful features on the image which are also scale invariant and, by using the SIFT descriptor, it becomes possible to track important points between frames. After finding the keypoints in an image, it is also possible to match these keypoints in the next image frame. **Keypoints** are important points in the image and useful information can be extracted by using them. OpenCV has good support for SIFT. Preprocessing means getting something ready for processing. It can include various types of substeps but the principle is always the same. We will now explain preprocessing and why it is important in a vision system. A small example of SIFT, sift.cpp can be found here:

```cpp
#include <opencv2/core/core.hpp>
#include <opencv2/highgui/highgui.hpp>
#include <opencv2/nonfree/features2d.hpp> //Thanks to Alessandro

using namespace cv;
int main(int argc, const char* argv[])
{
  const Mat input = imread(argv[1], CV_LOAD_IMAGE_GRAYSCALE);
//Load as grayscale

  SiftFeatureDetector detector;
  std::vector<KeyPoint> keypoints;
  detector.detect(input, keypoints);

  // Add results to image and save.
  Mat output;
  drawKeypoints(input, keypoints, output);
  imwrite("sift_result.png", output);

  return 0;
}
```

As you can see, the SIFT detector detects the `keypoints` in the following code line:

```
detector.detect(input, keypoints);
```

The drawing of the `keypoints` is done by the `drawKeypoints` function, shown here:

```
drawKeypoints(input, keypoints, output);
```

The output of this program for the library bookshelf image can be depicted as follows:

If you have trouble compiling the code on Ubuntu, you are probably missing the non-free OpenCV libraries. You can configure OpenCV with the `--enable-nonfree` option or you can install these libraries by entering the following commands to a terminal:

```
sudo add-apt-repository --yes ppa:xqms/opencv-nonfree
sudo apt-get update
sudo apt-get install libopencv-nonfree-dev
```

Using SURF

SURF is stands for **Speeded Up Robust Features (SURF)**. The weakness of SIFT is that it is a slow technique and here comes SURF as a fast feature extraction algorithm. SURF runs on an intermediate image representation called integral image, which is computed from the input image and is used to speed up the calculations in any rectangular area. OpenCV provides SURF functionalities in a very similar way to SIFT. To extract `keypoints` by using SURF, you can use the OpenCV SURF descriptor, as shown in the following code snippet:

```
int minHessian = 400;
SurfFeatureDetector detector( minHessian );
```

The rest is the same as with the SIFT example. SURF is often used in the feature extraction process, which must be done before the recognition phase.

To get more information on SURF, consult the OpenCV documentation, found at `http://docs.opencv.org/modules/nonfree/doc/feature_detection.html#surf`.

Using ORB

SIFT and SURF algorithms are very good at their job. But, because they are patented, it is necessary to make a payment for each year you use these algorithms. OpenCV has an efficient and free technique which is a good alternative to SIFT and SURF.

ORB stands for **Oriented FAST (Features from Accelerated Segment Test)** and Rotated BRIEF. ORB is a fusion of the FAST feature detector and the **Binary Robust Independent Elementary Features (BRIEF)** descriptor. Technically, it first uses FAST to extract keypoints and then applies a Harris corner detector to find the top keypoints among them. ORB is a modified algorithm that has also rotation invariance.

ORB was developed in the OpenCV labs and, as a consequence, the OpenCV library has a good implementation of it. The usage of ORB is very similar to SIFT and SURF.

For more information on ORB, consult the OpenCV documentation, found at `http://docs.opencv.org/2.4.9/modules/features2d/doc/feature_detection_and_description.html#orb`.

Using blob analysis

Blob analysis is an important technique for computer vision-based analysis of consistent image regions. It works really well for an application in which the objects being inspected are clearly discernible from the background. In the process of blob analysis, a **region** is any subset of pixels and a **blob** is a connected subset of pixels. By calculating the properties of blobs, it is possible to extract useful features and use this information for higher level operations like object detection.

As we'll handle blob analysis in the last chapter, try to understand the concept by reading more about the topic.

An important library for blob detection is cvBlobsLib which you can find at http://sourceforge.net/projects/cvblobslib/.

Summary

By now, we know how to extract meaningful features from vision data. Now you know how to summarize image data by extracting a small set of useful information and how to use this for higher level purposes. You also learned the strengths and weaknesses of feature extraction algorithms.

In this process you saw how higher level tasks like segmentation or detection can be done and, in the next chapter, we'll perform these higher level tasks! So, once again, please work on the example applications on feature detection to fully understand the topic and get ready for the intelligence of vision systems!

Recognition with OpenCV

6

This chapter is about the recognition methods used to arrive at a conclusion at the end of the vision process. Generally, a computer vision system extracts information from the sensor data and forms a decision such as detection, classification, or recognition. The decision comes after the feature extraction and is the recognition phase. This chapter will briefly explain the recognition process with a practical approach and you will also learn about the recognition capabilities of OpenCV, and much more! This chapter will enable you to write a brain for your vision-enabled application.

Building applications which can think

As humans, we make many decisions every day, pervasively. Although decision-making is an easy and natural process for the brain, it is not easy to enact those decisions. Owing to the fact that computers are strong at calculation but poor cognitively, the decision process then becomes a challenge. Even with all the challenges, enhancing cognitive ability with a vision application makes the job inspiring and exciting.

As in the feature extraction phase in the previous chapter, it would be a solution to use computational power to provide a solid basis for the decision-making process. It is helpful therefore to summarize vision data as inputs, and mathematically group decisions by using these inputs. It would then be possible to build vision applications which can take decisions mathematically.

Let's go over the most common cognitive computer vision terms—detection, classification, tracking, and recognition. **Detection** generally makes a basic decision on existence. If you remember the table-top object detection example in the previous chapter, there is one decision: to be or not to be. If no object is detected on the table, the algorithm concludes that table is empty. In this case, there are two classes of decision and this can also be thought of as a classification application with two basic classes. It is possible to develop more complex classification applications such as gesture recognition for five hand gestures. Here, the recognition of gestures can be made after the detection of the hand. As you can see, **recognition** is a more complex form of decision which generally lies over a detection algorithm and includes an identification phase. **Tracking** is also an important term concerning the detection of a particular object or event in one frame and then the identification of the same thing in all frames. Tracking can also be defined as the location of an object or event in a video stream over time. So, inter-frame relationships are needed in this process. Tracking is similar to detection and recognition, except for inter-frame relationships. Since recognition is a complex term, it will be used in the rest of the chapter to refer to all cognitive concepts.

OpenCV has good support for recognition which permits you to make a simple brain for your application. Even for the complex algorithms under the hood, it is made really simple and easy to use. In this chapter, we'll handle the most important cognitive techniques to enable vision applications to make decisions. The success of the recognition phase depends on the vision process. By using the information from previous chapters, this chapter will show you how to build smart vision applications with high recognition capabilities. OpenCV's object detection and machine learning libraries will help us a lot while implementing these recognition capabilities.

It is also possible to use third-party machine learning and pattern recognition libraries in your application. You can even write your own implementations to create classification, detection, recognition, tracking, and more. The benefit of using OpenCV's machine learning and object detection libraries is that it gives you optimized implementations for computer vision. But you always have the chance of adding to your vision application with third-party libraries wherever needed.

The same principles we talked about for images can be applied over the sensory data acquired by using Arduino. Moreover, it is not possible or effective to implement complex recognition algorithms in the Arduino environment due to the limits of resources. It is better to use the extracted sensory data from Arduino as the supplementary information to vision algorithms in order to improve the recognition performance of the computer vision application.

Template matching

A basic form of detection or recognition can be implemented by using a template which will be directly searched for in the image. Simply comparing the template to different areas in the image and finding the most similar (matching) regions in the template is a good way to implement template matching.

There are some techniques for finding the similarities between two image matrices. One of these techniques is to calculate the normalized cross correlation between images. Another technique is called square difference matching. There are many more techniques, but the best part is that you don't have to know the underlying complex calculation behind these techniques to be able to use them in your application. OpenCV has a useful function called `matchTemplate`, which provides you with many good options for template matching. This function `matchTemplate` takes the following arguments:

```
void matchTemplate(InputArray image, InputArray templ, OutputArray
result, int method)
```

This function's input is `image` and `templ` (template) and produces the resulting image as the map of comparison results. By using the method property, you can choose from six different template matching methods, including cross correlation and square difference matching.

> OpenCV has good documentation on template matching a good example application which you should see and try on your own. For the example application, visit the OpenCV documentation pages found at `http://docs.opencv.org/doc/tutorials/imgproc/histograms/template_matching/template_matching.html` and at `http://docs.opencv.org/modules/imgproc/doc/object_detection.html` location.

If you are searching for a given template, the `matchTemplate` function will help you a lot. But comparing images directly requires a lot of calculation, and it is not robust with image translations such as rotation and scaling. Here, in the following image, you can find an example of matching the Arduino image on the table top. The Arduino image is the template image and the table-top image is the input image which we search using the template. In this case, the image statistics of the Arduino image are compared with the image statistics of the sub-regions of the table-top image. The region which has the most similar image statistics to the Arduino image is marked as the matched template. As you can see, the Arduino is found on the table and a black rectangle is drawn around it:

Feature matching

Features are small sets of information extracted from images and they represent the image with less data. As we discussed in the previous chapter, it makes sense to use meaningful features of images instead of the whole matrix. The same principle can be applied to template matching. Instead of matching an image template, it would be better to match a template of a feature vector (or matrix) over the features of different image regions or different frames. Computational loads decrease if features are invariant against image transformations such as rotation, and scaling; template matching applied on features is also robust against image transformations.

In the previous chapter, it was argued that there are many ways of extracting useful features from images and it is possible to call these extracted features keypoints. OpenCV provides good mechanisms for keypoint matching and it makes sense to use them because of speed, robustness, and invariance with respect to scale and the rotation of techniques.

Let's use the OpenCV brute force matcher with SURF descriptors (useful features to describe an object or event) and find the Arduino on the table by using feature matching, as illustrated in this screenshot:

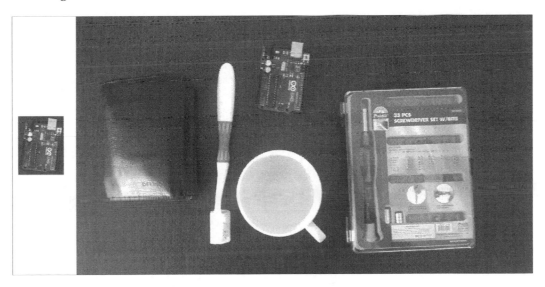

We want to find the Arduino on the tabletop. You can find the code for the tabletop_feature_matcher.cpp file here:

```cpp
#include <iostream>
#include "opencv2/core/core.hpp"
#include "opencv2/features2d/features2d.hpp"
#include "opencv2/highgui/highgui.hpp" #include "opencv2/nonfree/nonfree.hpp"

using namespace cv;
using namespace std;


int main(int argc, char** argv)
{
    if(argc != 3)
    {
        cout << "Usage:\n tabletop_feature_matcher
<image_to_match> <image_scene>\n" << endl;
        return -1;
    }

    Mat img_to_match = imread(argv[1], CV_LOAD_IMAGE_GRAYSCALE);
    Mat img_scene = imread(argv[2], CV_LOAD_IMAGE_GRAYSCALE);
    if(img_to_match.empty() || img_scene.empty())
    {
        printf("Can't read one of the images\n");
        return -1;
    }

    // detecting keypoints
    SurfFeatureDetector detector(400);
    vector<KeyPoint> keypoints1, keypoints2;
    detector.detect(img_to_match, keypoints1);
    detector.detect(img_scene, keypoints2);

    // computing descriptors
    SurfDescriptorExtractor extractor;
    Mat descriptors1, descriptors2;
    extractor.compute(img_to_match, keypoints1, descriptors1);
    extractor.compute(img_scene, keypoints2, descriptors2);

    // matching descriptors
    BFMatcher matcher(NORM_L2);
```

```
    vector<DMatch> matches;
    matcher.match(descriptors1, descriptors2, matches);

    // drawing the results
    namedWindow("matches", 1);
    Mat img_matches;
    drawMatches(img_to_match, keypoints1, img_scene, keypoints2,
matches, img_matches);
    imshow("matches", img_matches);
    imwrite("matches.png",img_matches);
    waitKey(0);

    return 0;
}
```

After you compile the code, you can run it with two image filename arguments, and they are the image which will be searched for (the template), and the scene image. For example, on Windows you can type:

```
tabletop_feature_matcher.exe template.png scene.png
```

If need be, you should change the filenames. After running this command, you can see that it will match the keypoints in two images, as shown here:

You can see that the keypoints on the Arduino are perfectly matched in the scene. Do not forget that it is possible to use different feature detectors as introduced in the previous chapter. Now let's go through the new parts of the code and explain them in a clear manner to reinforce the matching process.

Firstly, the SURF feature detector is defined with the hessian value `400` and two keypoint vectors are defined for two images. The hessian value is basically a sensitivity parameter that adjusts how important a keypoint must be, and therefore it will affect the number of keypoints which are found. A larger hessian value will result in a few but more salient keypoints, whereas a smaller value will result in more numerous but less salient keypoints. Then the `detect` method is invoked to get keypoints from two input images, as shown in this code snippet:

```
SurfFeatureDetector detector(400);
vector<KeyPoint> keypoints1, keypoints2;
detector.detect(img_to_match, keypoints1);
detector.detect(img_scene, keypoints2);
```

In the next step, descriptors are extracted from these keypoints by using the SURF descriptor extractor, as shown here:

```
// computing descriptors
SurfDescriptorExtractor extractor;
Mat descriptors1, descriptors2;
extractor.compute(img_to_match, keypoints1, descriptors1);
extractor.compute(img_scene, keypoints2, descriptors2);
```

The brute force matcher is then used to match the features computed by the SURF descriptor extractor. Then, these matches are saved in the `matches` vector. The brute force matcher takes the descriptor of one feature in the set and tries to match it with all other features in the second set using distance calculations. The closest calculation is taken to be a match, as illustrated in the following code:

```
BFMatcher matcher(NORM_L2);
vector<DMatch> matches;
matcher.match(descriptors1, descriptors2, matches);
```

The rest of the code just displays the matches and saves the matches image as `matches.png`:

```
    namedWindow("matches", 1);
    Mat img_matches;
    drawMatches(img_to_match, keypoints1, img_scene, keypoints2,
matches, img_matches);
    imshow("matches", img_matches);
    imwrite("matches.png",img_matches);
```

As was discussed previously, it is easy to use different feature detectors, descriptor extractors, and matchers. Different methods of feature matching will be discussed later in the chapter.

FLANN-based matching

FLANN stands for **Fast Library for Approximate Nearest Neighbors**. It contains a collection of algorithms optimized for a fast nearest-neighbor search. It works faster than the brute force matcher, especially with bigger datasets.

 OpenCV also contains a FLANN-based matcher and a good sample application which uses the FLANN matcher. It is a good idea to try it! You can find the FLANN matcher tutorial on the OpenCV documentation page at `http://docs.opencv.org/doc/tutorials/features2d/feature_flann_matcher/feature_flann_matcher.html`.

When you run the FLANN matcher example for our table-top Arduino scene, you will see that it finds the matched features of images faster than brute force matching. Here, you can see the output of the FLANN matcher code:

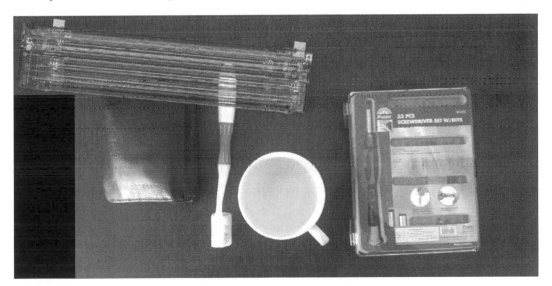

Another good and comprehensive application can be found in the OpenCV samples directory with the filename `descriptor_extractor_matcher.cpp`. This example comprehensively handles all kinds of descriptors, extractors and matchers supported by OpenCV. You can compile and try different descriptors, extractors, matchers and then compare the results! The file can be found in this directory `opencv\sources\samples\cpp\`.

Using cascade classifiers

Extracting keypoints from an image and trying to match them with a certain template is a good way of finding certain matches in an image. But what if we want to solve more general problems such as human detection or face detection? In this case, since every human has a different face, the nature of the application requires more generalization. To classify areas of an image as a face, for example, much more complex classification mechanisms are needed. Cascaded classifiers give us the opportunity to build complex classifiers by mixing simple classifiers in a cascaded architecture. It is then possible to solve more complex problems such as fruit recognition or face detection.

Classifiers can also be classified as supervised, unsupervised, and partially supervised. This taxonomy is about the learning method of the classifier. In supervised learning, you teach the classifier what is true and what is not. This is done via true samples and false samples. For example, if you want to teach your classifiers to detect the human eye, you provide real eye photos as true samples, and other photos which are not eyes as false samples, by labeling each sample as true or false. Then, the classifier adapts or learns the patterns of the eye by improving the weights of the extracted features in each sample.

OpenCV provides good classification interfaces and even cascaded classifiers. Cascaded classifiers are useful for solving many problems. Training the classifier with a good input sample set (training set) helps cascaded classifiers to solve hard problems such as object detection, and recognition. A good example application comes with the OpenCV samples and there is also a pretrained face detector which you can use in your applications. In OpenCV, training data is generally stored in the XML files and it is easy to load these XML files and use them in your application.

In OpenCV cascade classifiers, object detection can be made with the `detectMultiScale` function; this function has the following form:

```
void CascadeClassifier::detectMultiScale(const Mat& image,
vector<Rect>& objects, double scaleFactor=1.1, int minNeighbors=3,
int flags=0, Size minSize=Size(), Size maxSize=Size())
```

A good example can be found in the OpenCV C++ samples. Refer to this directory `opencv\sources\samples\cpp\tutorial code\ objectDetection` and the files `objectDetection.cpp` and `objectDetection2.cpp`. The required XML files are located under `opencv\sources\data\haarcascades` and `opencv\sources\ data\lbpcascades`. There is also a tutorial page on OpenCV documentation which explains face detection with cascaded classifiers, found at `http://docs.opencv.org/doc/tutorials/objdetect/ cascade_classifier/cascade_classifier.html`.

It is also possible to train cascaded classifiers for your own detection application cases. OpenCV comes with two applications to train cascaded classifiers — `opencv_ haartraining` and `opencv_traincascade`. The `opencv_createsamples` utility can be used to create negative and positive samples. All of these utilities are located in the OpenCV's `bin` folders.

OpenCV has a good documentation page for training cascade classifiers, found at `http://docs.opencv.org/doc/user_guide/ug_ traincascade.html`. Please follow the tutorials on the documentation page to implement a detection algorithm for your favorite fruit!

Another good example in the OpenCV documentation is face recognition with cascade classifiers. OpenCV has prebuilt face recognizer models such as the Fischer face recognizer model. And it is easy to recognize faces by using the predict method of the model, and. The example application and explanation can be found on the OpenCV documentation page at `http://docs.opencv.org/modules/contrib/doc/facerec/ tutorial/facerec_video_recognition.html`.

Using support vector machines

A **support vector machine (SVM)** is a classifier formally defined by separating a hyperplane. A hyperplane is simply a separation line between classes. When you group data with feature values in a multidimensional feature space, SVM separates the hyperplane and, in this process, each separated group is concluded as a class. It is possible to divide a dividable feature space in many ways. The problem is to get optimal separation between classes.

Originally, SVM was a technique for building an optimal binary classifier. Later, the technique was extended to deal with regression and clustering problems by separating spaces even with non-linear separation. In practice, SVM is good for optimally classifying the feature space. You can solve complex classification problems with SVM.

To be able to use SVM, it is mandatory to understand the separation principle. A good graphical representation of linearly separable classes can be found on the OpenCV documentation page. In the following image, you can find the feature space image from the OpenCV documentation page, with two classes (red rectangles and blue circles) and possibly, lines (green lines) to separate them. The green line is the decision boundary or hyperplane. If it is possible to divide the feature space with a single straight line, then the data is called linearly separable:

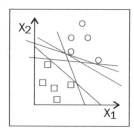

Finding the optimal line to provide the optimal classification of the samples is a difficult problem, and this is what SVM is used for. Optimal separation is only possible by setting the maximum margin between the hyperplane and the closest samples. This also provides the maximum amount of immunity against noises. Please see the optimal separation in the following image:

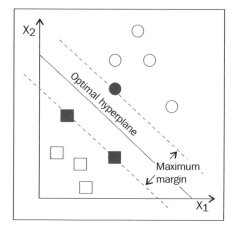

An advantage of SVM is that you don't need the whole dataset to train the classifier. Only samples closer to the decision boundary will train the SVM. Here, the filled rectangles and filled circle are called support planes. They are used to find the decision boundary. In this process, it becomes possible to reduce data in training to include only the support planes. Once SVM is trained, it can classify new data by using the optimal hyperplane. Non-linear separation in more complex feature spaces is also possible with SVM but, as the concept is the same, we won't take it any further.

To train the SVM classifier, the following method can be used:

```
bool CvSVM::train(const Mat& trainData, const Mat& responses,
const Mat& varIdx=Mat(), const Mat& sampleIdx=Mat(), CvSVMParams
params=CvSVMParams() )
```

And to predict the classification output, you can use the `predict` method:

```
float CvSVM::predict(const Mat& sample, bool returnDFVal=false )
const
```

> A simple but good SVM classifier example application is explained in the OpenCV documentation pages found at http://docs.opencv.org/ doc/tutorials/ml/introduction_to_svm/introduction_to_ svm.html.
>
> Try to run the example application, then change the parameters and see the results. More general documentation of SVM implementation in OpenCV can be found at http://docs.opencv.org/2.4.9/ modules/ml/doc/support_vector_machines.html.
>
> OpenCV also has a SVM example application for non-linearly separable data. You can find the example in the documentation page at http:// docs.opencv.org/doc/tutorials/ml/non_linear_svms/non_ linear_svms.html.

Summary

In this chapter, you learned about the philosophy behind the recognition process, and how to use it in your OpenCV application! You have also learned the most common techniques for detection and recognition. So you now have an idea of how to approach such problems.

Machine learning is a big topic about which many books have been written. But, once you get the idea and get some hands-on practice you will be well placed. This will enable you to solve very complex problems.

Recognition will also be handled in the last chapter with real life example. So try to understand the idea behind recognition and read the OpenCV documentation on machine learning, video, and object detection modules. This will help you to comprehend all of these concepts and use the techniques for your own application!

The next step is communication between Arduino and OpenCV. Get ready for the next chapter!

7

Communicating with Arduino Using OpenCV

We have discussed computer vision topics from data acquisition to recognition. We also discussed how to collect sensor data from the environment. Now it is time to establish a solid link between devices. A communication line between Arduino and the computer is needed to be able to combine the sensor data with computer vision. This link is also required to turn the conclusion of the computer vision process into physical output. In this chapter, we will discuss communication between Arduino and the computer. We will also look at the best practices of information exchange between the devices. This chapter will help you to design a robust communication channel between Arduino and an intelligent agent. Both wired and wireless communication interfaces will be dealt with. You will observe that, beyond the physical connection, the idea behind the information exchange and information modeling is very important.

Communicating with Arduino

Arduino Uno R3 is a development board which is built with an ATmega328 microcontroller. The communication capabilities of Arduino Uno R3 are dependent on the capabilities of the ATmega328 microcontroller. Because the ATmega328 has a **Serial Peripheral Interface (SPI)** and a **Universal Synchronous Asynchronous Receiver Transmitter (USART)** module in its hardware, it offers great communication opportunities to its users.

One of the most important strengths of Arduino is it's huge community support and free software libraries for various shields and modules. Arduino Uno has a rich set of supported communication shields which give the user the opportunity to pick the most appropriate communication shield for the target application. The union of shields and software libraries speed up the prototyping of applications dramatically.

With a system level approach it is possible to say that communication interface is required for information transfer between devices. In this scheme, both Arduino and the vision controller should agree on the physical properties and the content of data transfer. When Arduino sends the sensor information to the vision controller, the vision controller should know the format of the data to be able to understand it. This consensus is possible via a communication protocol at the application level. By implementing such a good communication protocol, it is possible to transfer the data in an efficient way. Such an application level communication protocol will be handled in this chapter. The best part is that you can use this communication protocol in any physical communication interface, wired or wireless. So, the application level communication will be hardware independent. It means that, with the same software, it is possible to send information via a wired or wireless connection.

In a two way communication scheme, both the Arduino system and the vision controller should be able to pack the data into a message before sending it. Similarly, it is necessary to parse the received protocol message to retrieve the data inside the message. This means that a message packer and a message parser implementation are needed. In this chapter you will learn how to implement these communication capabilities on both Arduino and the vision controller.

While communicating with Arduino using OpenCV, we need to think about the communication capabilities of both platforms. Naturally, both must work on the same type of communication channel. The easiest way of connecting Arduino to a computer or a microcomputer is by using the **Universal Serial Bus (USB)** interface.

Normally, while USART is very simple, USB is a complex communication line, but Arduino Uno uses the **Virtual COM Port (VCP)** USB profile which makes communication really easy! The VCP driver allows the computer to make the USB behave like a serial COM port. In the hardware, the USART pins of the ATmega328 are connected to a USART to USB-VCP convertor **Integrated Circuit (IC)** and all the conversions are done via this IC. With Arduino's hardware architecture you can write simple serial port codes and all the data will be sent over the USB cable. When you plug the USB cable into your computer, the VCP driver will be activated and your operating system will detect the Arduino as a VCP device. This means you can write simple serial port software to communicate with Arduino.

To be able to reduce software complexity, different types of USART converters (such as VCP) are used to be able to establish different kinds of communication channels. It is possible to communicate via **Bluetooth Low Energy (BLE)** by using a BLE module with a USART interface. In this case, when you send anything over the USART interface which is connected to the BLE module, data will be transmitted over BLE. The same is true for ZigBee communication. The XBee module (which is a ZigBee module) can be connected to the Arduino over the USART interface and, when you configure XBee correctly and send data over the USART interface, data will be sent with the ZigBee protocol. This generic mechanism makes life really easy in terms of software programming.

Now, let's go through the vision controller part of the connection. As you know, OpenCV is a multiplatform library. This means that it can run on various operating systems. This fact also indicates that the communication software can run on any one of these platforms. Because of this, the communication software on the vision controller is implemented by using Java. Moreover, you will see that the software is generic and if you want to work with .NET or another framework you can easily switch to it.

Now, let's go through all these topics and get ready for hands-on applications!

Wired communications

In this part we'll handle the most common Arduino wired communication interfaces with a practical approach. You can choose which medium best fits for your application!

Communicating via USB

The easiest way of communicating with Arduino is by using the built-in USB serial interface. By using serial communication, it is possible to exchange data between the Arduino board and other devices such as computers with serial communication capability. Serial means that one byte at a time is transmitted and, while this may seem slow, it is a very common and relatively easy way to transmit data.

All Arduinos have at least one serial interface. Serial communication is done via the USART module, as was explained previously. The Arduino Uno digital pins 0 and 1 are connected to an integrated IC which converts the signals to USB. In this case, pin 0 is used for **RX (receive)**, and pin 1 is used for **TX (transmit)**. Hence, you cannot use these pins for digital I/O if you use them for serial communication.

The Arduino Uno USB interface works with the Virtual COM Port profile. So, just plug one end of the USB cable into your Arduino and the other into your computer and you will get a working communication channel. That's so easy!

Of course, simply establishing the channel won't make the devices exchange information. Data transfer is required to exchange information. Let's send `Hello World!` to Arduino and monitor it in the computer by using the Arduino IDE. Open a new sketch in the Arduino IDE, paste the simple `Hello World` code in the sketch and upload it to your Arduino Uno R3:

```
void setup() {
  Serial.begin(9600);
}

void loop() {
    Serial.println("Hello World!");
    delay(1000);
}
```

The preceding code will send one `Hello World!` message to the computer per second. Before receiving the message from computer, let's go through this simple code.

```
Serial.begin(9600);
```

The `Serial.begin` method is used to start the serial communication with a specific baud rate. The baud rate defines the data transfer rate of serial communication. In this case we have started the serial port at `9600` baud. In this case, Arduino will send 9600 symbols per second to transfer the message. It is possible to adjust the baud rate, usually to one of several predefined options. However, it is important that both the Arduino and the computer use the same baud rate; otherwise the communication will be gibberish. Let's go through this simple code.

```
Serial.println("Hello World!");
```

The `Serial.println` method is used to send a string over a serial port. In this case, a simple `Hello World` message is sent. To be able to capture this message by using the Arduino IDE, firstly verify if the right serial port is selected. You can verify it from **Arduino IDE | Tools | Serial Port**. If everything is okay, in the Arduino IDE, click on the menu item **Tools | Serial Monitor** and the serial monitor will be opened, as shown in this screenshot:

But this communication is only one way. Normally it is possible to send data from Arduino IDE's serial monitor, but the sketch which we load to the Arduino is not yet capable of receiving the data over a serial line. So, let's improve the capabilities of Arduino for two-way communication. Arduino should understand a specific set of commands and it should react to each command in a meaningful way. Here, in the code, you can find the required sketch:

```
String inputString = ""; /* a string to hold incoming data */
boolean stringComplete = false; /* whether the string is complete
*/
int led = 13;

void setup() {
  /* initialize the digital pin as an output. */
  pinMode(led, OUTPUT);
  /* initialize serial: */
  Serial.begin(9600);
  /* reserve 256 bytes for the inputString: */
  inputString.reserve(256);
  Serial.println("Arduino: I am ready!");
}
```

```
void loop() {
  /* print the string when a newline arrives: */
  if (stringComplete) {
    Serial.println("Sir: " + inputString);
    if(inputString=="Hello Arduino!")
    {
      Serial.println("Arduino: Hello Sir!");
    }
    else if(inputString == "How are you?" )
    {
      Serial.println("Arduino: Fine thanks, and you?");
    }
    else if(inputString == "Fine!" )
    {
      Serial.println("Arduino: This makes me happy sir!");
    }
    else if(inputString == "Light up your LED!" )
    {
      Serial.println("Arduino: Surely Sir!");
      digitalWrite(led, HIGH);
    }
    else if(inputString == "Light down your LED!" )
    {
      Serial.println("Arduino: Surely Sir!");
      digitalWrite(led, LOW);
    }
    else if(inputString == "Goodbye Arduino!" )
    {
      Serial.println("Arduino: Goodbye Sir!");
    }
    else
    {
      Serial.println("Arduino: I cannot understand you Sir!");
    }
    /* clear the string: */
    inputString = "";
    stringComplete = false;
  }
}

/*
SerialEvent occurs whenever a new data comes in the
 hardware serial RX. This routine is run between each
 time loop() runs, so using delay inside loop can delay
```

```
  response. Multiple bytes of data may be available.
  */
void serialEvent() {
  while (Serial.available()) {
    /* get the new byte: */
    char inChar = (char)Serial.read();
    /* add it to the inputString: */
    inputString += inChar;
    /*if the incoming character is a newline, set a flag
     so the main loop can do something about it: */
    if (inChar == '!' || inChar == '?') {
      stringComplete = true;
    }
  }
}
```

Now let's explain how this event-driven code works:

```
String inputString = "";
boolean stringComplete = false;
int led = 13;
```

Firstly, we create the `inputString` variable to store incoming data and `stringComplete` to indicate the completion of the reception of the string. Lastly, we assign `led = 13` to use with the `digital.write` method to light it up and down. Here is the remaining part of the code:

```
void setup() {
  pinMode(led, OUTPUT);
  Serial.begin(9600);
  inputString.reserve(256);
  Serial.println("Arduino: I am ready!");
}
```

In the `setup` function, we initialize the LED pin as output with the `pinMode` function to turn it on and off in the loop. After that, the serial port baud rate is set and a welcoming message is sent, `Arduino: I am ready!`

It is better to emphasize the difference between this code and the simple code given prior to this code. The `serialEvent` function introduces event-driven usage to capture incoming messages, as shown here:

```
void serialEvent() {
  while (Serial.available()) {

    char inChar = (char)Serial.read();
```

```
      inputString += inChar;
      if (inChar == '!' || inChar == '?') {
        stringComplete = true;
      }
    }
  }
```

Whenever a new string enters the RX line of your Arduino, the listening function `serialEvent` starts to record an incoming string from your computer. Every character is added one after another to the `inputString` variable. The condition, `if (inChar == '!' || inChar == '?')`, checks whether the incoming string is finished. If the condition is satisfied, the `stringComplete` flag is set to `true`, which will be used in the main loop. Now, let's jump to the main body of the code:

```
void loop() {
  if (stringComplete) {
    Serial.println("Sir:" + inputString);
    if(inputString=="Hello Arduino!")
    {
      Serial.println("Arduino: Hello Sir!");
    }
    else if(inputString == "How are you?" )
    {
      Serial.println("Arduino: Fine thanks, and you?");
    }
    else if(inputString == "Fine!" )
    {
      Serial.println("Arduino: This makes me happy sir!");
    }
    else if(inputString == "Light up your LED!" )
    {
      Serial.println("Arduino: Surely Sir!");
      digitalWrite(led, HIGH);
    }
    else if(inputString == "Light down your LED!" )
    {
      Serial.println("Arduino: Surely Sir!");
      digitalWrite(led, LOW);
    }
    else if(inputString == "Goodbye Arduino!" )
    {
      Serial.println("Arduino: Goodbye Sir!");
    }
```

```
      else
      {
        Serial.println("Arduino: I cannot understand you Sir!");
      }

      inputString = "";
      stringComplete = false;
    }
  }
```

At the top, the `if` statement checks if the `stringComplete` flag is set to `true` or `false`. When it is set to `true`, the code checks what we have sent through the serial line. If the string we have sent from the serial monitor matches any string in the `if` statements, the code replies with an appropriate answer. Otherwise, it sends the string, `I can not understand you Sir!`. After each string is read, the `stringComplete` flag is set to `false` and `inputString` is set to an empty string. Arduino actually drives the LED and is remotely controlled via the serial line for light up LED and light down LED commands. Similarly, it is possible to trigger a sensor measurement and send the value back via the serial line.

Here, you can find the output of the conversation window:

Communicating via the serial port

As we mentioned before, serial port usage is very common with the Arduino. Sometimes our project may require more than one serial communication line. Since Arduino Uno has only one built-in USART line, we need to look for alternative ways to mimic serial communication. Luckily, the Arduino Software Serial Library gives us the ability to convert any pair of pins into RX and TX pins.

 For more information on the Arduino Software Serial Library, visit the Arduino reference page at http://www.arduino.cc/en/ Reference/SoftwareSerial. Also, note that the example sketch on this reference page is included with the Arduino IDE.

To get the essence of the library, let's go over a case where we connect our Arduino to the PC to log the data of incoming data streams via the BLE module. The easiest way to connect a communication module (in this case, the BLE module) is to connect the Arduino USART interface. Without getting desperate, any two possible pairs of pins can be assigned as the RX and TX for the BLE module! You can even use the same code for XBee as the BLE module! The only thing you should do is correctly connect the module pins to the Arduino. The same code will work for both.

Now, let's go through the Software Serial Library example given on the Arduino examples page to assist communication in your project:

```
/*
   Software serial multple serial test

   Receives from the hardware serial, sends to software serial.
   Receives from software serial, sends to hardware serial.

   The circuit:
   * RX is digital pin 10 (connect to TX of other device)
   * TX is digital pin 11 (connect to RX of other device)

   Note:
   Not all pins on the Mega and Mega 2560 support change interrupts,
   so only the following can be used for RX:
   10, 11, 12, 13, 50, 51, 52, 53, 62, 63, 64, 65, 66, 67, 68, 69

   Not all pins on the Leonardo support change interrupts,
   so only the following can be used for RX:
   8, 9, 10, 11, 14 (MISO), 15 (SCK), 16 (MOSI).
```

```
created back in the mists of time
modified 25 May 2012
by Tom Igoe
based on Mikal Hart's example

This example code is in the public domain.

*/
#include <SoftwareSerial.h>

SoftwareSerial mySerial(10, 11); // RX, TX

void setup()
{
  // Open serial communications and wait for port to open:
  Serial.begin(57600);
  while (!Serial) {
    ; // wait for serial port to connect. Needed for Leonardo only
  }

  Serial.println("Goodnight moon!");

  // set the data rate for the SoftwareSerial port
  mySerial.begin(4800);
  mySerial.println("Hello, world?");
}

void loop() // run over and over
{
  if (mySerial.available())
    Serial.write(mySerial.read());
  if (Serial.available())
    mySerial.write(Serial.read());
}
```

The code basically exchanges data between the hardware and the serial port. Let's start from the head of the code:

```
#include <SoftwareSerial.h>

SoftwareSerial mySerial(10, 11); // RX, TX
```

As seen in the preceding code, the Software Serial Library header is added. Then, the new software serial is created with the RX and TX pins 10 and 11, respectively:

```
void setup()
{
// Open serial communications and wait for port to open:
Serial.begin(57600);
while (!Serial) {
 ; // wait for serial port to connect. Needed for Leonardo only
}


Serial.println("Goodnight moon!");

// set the data rate for the SoftwareSerial port
mySerial.begin(4800);
mySerial.println("Hello, world?");
}
```

As usual, the setup() function calls the necessary settings for serial communication. Let's clarify the difference between the Serial and mySerial objects. Serial is the normal built-in serial port, communicating at 57600 baud. The MySerial object is the software object that we are creating, communicating at 4800 baud. Each serial port is started and sends the debug messages, Goodnight moon! and Hello, world?, respectively. Here is the remaining code:

```
void loop() // run over and over
{
if (mySerial.available())
  Serial.write(mySerial.read());
if (Serial.available())
  mySerial.write(Serial.read());
}
```

The loop function of the code transfers messages coming from the other serial port. When the software serial mySerial object gets a message, it sends it to the hardware serial port. Similarly, the hardware serial port sends the data to the software serial. The drawing given here illustrates the schematic:

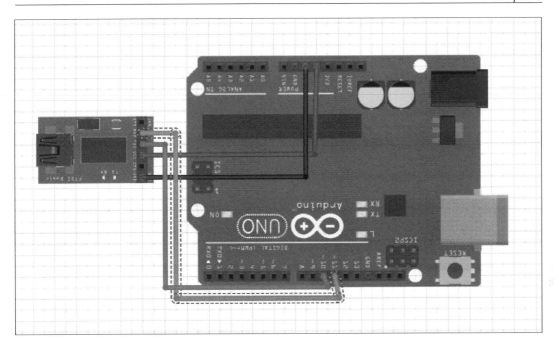

With any FTDI module, as can be seen from the drawing, a software serial example can be implemented and an exchange of data can be observed by using any serial port listener application such as the Hercules SETUP utility. The FTDI module is a module which converts USART to USB with Virtual COM Port.

> You can download and evaluate the Hercules SETUP utility from the webpage at http://www.hw-group.com/products/hercules/index_en.html. It is an extremely powerful communication tool which also supports serial port communication.

Communicating via Ethernet

Ethernet is a family of networking technologies. With the Ethernet function on your Arduino, you can also exchange data from anywhere, by using the Internet connection. There are plenty of application possibilities, such as controlling a robot over a web page or getting an e-mail when an intruder image is captured while you are not at home! Arduino Ethernet Shield gives you the ability to connect your Arduino to the Internet or any Ethernet-based network. The following screenshot shows the Arduino board on the left with the Ethernet Shield on the right:

For more information on the Arduino Ethernet Shield, visit the Arduino product page at http://www.arduino.cc/en/ Main/ArduinoEthernetShield.

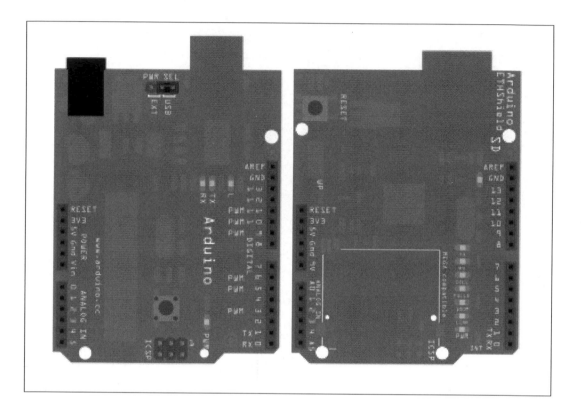

Wireless communications

After introducing common wired communication protocols, this section will introduce common wireless communication interfaces for the Arduino. Again we intend to be practical while introducing wireless technologies. Wireless modules are important in terms of mobility. You will inevitably use wireless communication modules if you are working on a mobile robot.

Communicating via Bluetooth Low Energy

Bluetooth is a wireless technology standard for data exchange over short distances. It is one of the most common wireless protocols among gadgets. We can see Bluetooth connectivity both in smartphones and house appliances. With Bluetooth modules, it is possible to exchange data at up to 100 meters.

Bluetooth Low Energy, or Bluetooth Smart, has much less power consumption while maintaining a similar communication range. Low power consumption is very important for mobile applications since the required energy is taken from the onboard battery. Energy consumption becomes especially important when there is a high rate of data transmission and a lot of distance from the source. Both cases tend to consume more battery than usual. So, be conscious of this when selecting your Bluetooth module. We would like to introduce two popular **Bluetooth Low Energy (BLE)** modules. The first one is RedBearLab's shield. There is a lot of support for applications both for Arduino and the BLE device. The development of any application is very simple with this shield.

Getting into BLE is beyond the scope of this chapter. If you are interested in using BLE connectivity, feel free to look for solutions. Keep in mind that using a module which uses a serial port for communication with the Arduino makes your BLE integration much easier, as we mentioned earlier in this chapter. Remember, the following link is a good start for BLE!

 For more information on Bluetooth Low Power Arduino shield, visit the RedBearLab page at `http://redbearlab.com/bleshield/`.

Here is the picture of the Bluetooth Low Power Arduino shield:

Communicating via ZigBee

In common with Bluetooth and BLE, ZigBee is a high-level communication protocol for creating personal networks. Devices that have ZigBee protocols can send data over long distances by passing data through a mesh network. Data is transmitted over intermediate ZigBee nodes to the distant nodes. It is typically used for low power applications. XBee is a product which can be loaded with the ZigBee protocol. They are cost-efficient connectivity devices. Applications such as sensor networks which require relatively long-range connectivity are suitable for use with XBee modules. XBee modules can talk with Arduino via serial. Just like BLE, serial port communication can be used for easy integration.

The Arduino XBee shield is what we will propose as the wireless connectivity solution. The Arduino Wireless SD shield page overviews the product which is intended to be used for XBee.

 For more information on Arduino Wireless SD Shield, please visit the Arduino product page at http://www.arduino.cc/en/Main/ArduinoWirelessShield.

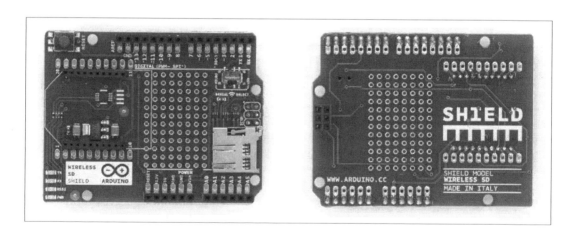

Communicating via Wi-Fi

Wi-Fi is a local networking technology. Wi-Fi modules not only give us the ability to connect devices to the Internet, but are also suitable for local communication. Note that, by using Wi-Fi connectivity, you can control a robot miles away by accessing it over the Internet. Just don't forget to connect your robot to a local Wi-Fi network! It is possible to make a robot which wanders around the home and keeps sending snapshots of your home while wandering around rooms.

We will introduce you to Arduino Wi-Fi Shield to use for any kind of wireless robotics application which will connect over Wi-Fi. Wi-Fi is best used when higher communication speed is needed. It also allows you to connect to higher level wireless networks such as the Internet. Wireless connection to the Internet will make your application more exciting. If you need to connect your Arduino to the Internet without wires, it is best to use the Wi-Fi shield. You can see the link to the well-documented Arduino Wi-Fi Shield page in the box. This product page has tutorials which show how to use this shield in your applications.

 For more information on Arduino Wi-Fi Shield, visit the Arduino product page at http://www.arduino.cc/en/Main/ArduinoWiFiShield.

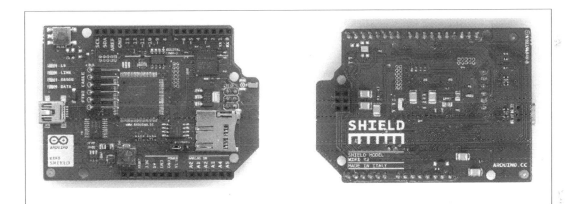

Communicating via radio frequency

Radio Frequency (RF) communication is one of the most common wireless communication interfaces. It is possible to establish different kinds of radio networks by using RF transceiver modules. RF transceivers are really cheap and they are easy to use.

The NRF24L01 from Nordic Semiconductors is a very cheap and robust RF transceiver and it supports a number of channel frequencies in the 2.4 GHz band. NRF24L series RF transceivers are widely used in various types of Arduino-based applications.

We will examine NRF24L series transceivers thoroughly in the last chapter, with an example application. You can look at the documentation pages to get more information about this module. The following screenshot shows you what the NRF24L series RF transceivers looks similar to:

 The available Arduino libraries for interfacing the NRF24L01 are documented in the Arduino page and can be found at http://playground.arduino.cc/InterfacingWithHardware/Nrf24L01. You can find more documentation on the Nordic Semiconductor product page at http://www.nordicsemi.com/eng/Products/2.4GHz-RF/nRF24L01P.

Communicating with Java

Arduino IDE has a serial monitor which can be used to communicate with Arduino in a simple but restricted way. Many computer vision applications need automated and specialized communication architecture. Imagine that you want to run a face detection algorithm when the user presses a button. This is the doorbell button triggered face detection application which we discussed in previous chapters. In this case, the Arduino should send the button pressed information to the vision controller and the communication controller should start the face detection algorithm. You have learned how to send button press information over the serial port, but the missing part is how to understand this message and invoke the face detection algorithm in the vision controller.

Another use case is sending the output or the decision of the vision controller to the Arduino system and making the Arduino react. In the face recognition application which is triggered by the doorbell button, the vision controller should send a verification message to the Arduino system and then the Arduino system should open the door by driving an inductor or motor.

In both cases, the vision controller's communication software should be integrated with the computer vision software. This requires custom software for the communication line. There must also be automatic communication between the Arduino and the vision controller.

As OpenCV is a multiplatform application, there are many other options available for the development of communication software. With Windows, it is possible to use Visual C++ to integrate visual capabilities, and Windows communication libraries can be used for serial communication. In this case, a unified application can be developed as a single executable. Another alternative for Windows is using C# and .NET to build both the user interface and the communication. If you have developed your vision application with C++, you can either build it as a library or use this library in the C# application to get vision functionality. Alternatively, you can build your OpenCV application as a standalone executable and then invoke this executable from the C# (.NET) application which manages the communication. These specific solutions only work with Windows.

Java can be used for a multiplatform solution. More or less the same architectures which we discussed for Windows can be implemented with Java. Because of this, Java is preferred as the development environment for communication software on the vision controller. Remember that OpenCV has a Java API which enables you to develop everything including the vision algorithms, communication software and the user interfaces in one platform. Alternatively, you can call your vision application executable, developed in any OpenCV API, from the Java application which is responsible for user interaction and/or communication management.

We'll develop our own serial terminal with Java, and learn how to customize it to automate our vision tasks, to present a generic application for communication capabilities. Java has several libraries for serial communication. The RXTX library is a commonly used serial communication library which simplifies serial communication. Keeping applications as simple as possible will make the idea easier to understand. So, let's build our own serial communication software with Java! It will work in any environment.

> You can go to the RXTX library webpage for more information. The home page for the RXTX library is http://rxtx.qbang.org/. You can download the pre-built RXTX libraries for multiple platforms from http://rxtx.qbang.org/wiki/index.php/Download.

Before getting started, you should install the **Java Development Kit (JDK)**. The important thing is that the JDK platform and the RXTX platform are the same. If you installed JDK for x86 platforms, the x86 RXTX library should also be downloaded. To avoid inconsistencies, we suggest using both the JDK and RXTX library for x86/i368 platforms.

In this application we used version 2.1-7, which is the stable version of the RXTX library, and JDK 1.8.0 for x86. The development IDE is Eclipse Luna for Java developers for x86 (32-bit) platforms. As was stressed before, installing the JDK, Eclipse, and RXTX library for 32-bit platforms won't affect anything else and it will prevent inconsistencies. Please go through these steps:

 You can download the correct version of the RXTX library files from
`http://rxtx.qbang.org/pub/rxtx/rxtx-2.1-7-bins-r2.zip`.

1. Now open Eclipse for Java developers. In the menu, go to **File | New | Java Project**.

2. For the project name, write `java_serial` and select the JRE as **Use Default JRE**. For the project layout, select the option **Create separate folders for sources and class files** as illustrated in the following screenshot:

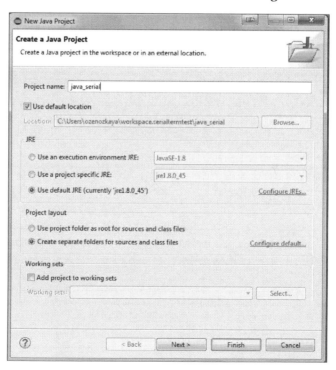

3. Then click on the **Next** button.

4. After clicking the **Next** button, the Java settings screen will be opened.

5. Click the libraries tab and press the button for **Add External JARs...**.

6. Then browse to the folder in which you have downloaded and extracted the RXTX library and select the RXTXcomm.jar.

7. Then click the Open button. It should be added to the list, as illustrated as in the following screenshot:

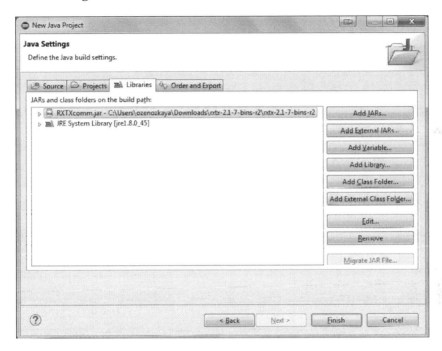

8. Click the **Finish** button to go to the project development screen in Eclipse.

9. Then go the the rxtx library folder and navigate to the Windows\i368-mingw32 folder. Copy rxtxSerial.dll and paste it into the C:\Windows\System32 folder.

10. And, in your Eclipse project, right-click RXTXComm.jar, go to **Properties | Native Library** and click **External Folder...**.

11. In this window, go to the rxtx directory and navigate to Windows/i368-mingw32.

12. Then click the **Ok** button and apply the changes by pressing **Apply** and then **Ok**. Now you are ready for the next step.

13. Since the codes are a little bit long, we prefer to share them via GitHub. You can download the files from `https://github.com/ozenozkaya/arduino_cv_serial_java`. There are two files called `SerialComm.java` and `SerialTerminal.java`. Drag and drop both files into the `src` folder in your Eclipse project and copy them to your project. In this case your project will look as follows:

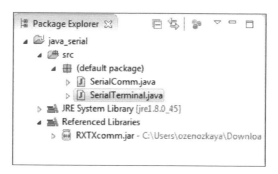

14. Connect your Arduino Uno R3 to your computer and right-click your Eclipse project `java_serial`. Then select **Run As | Java Application | Serial Terminal** (the default package). You will see the terminal application running:

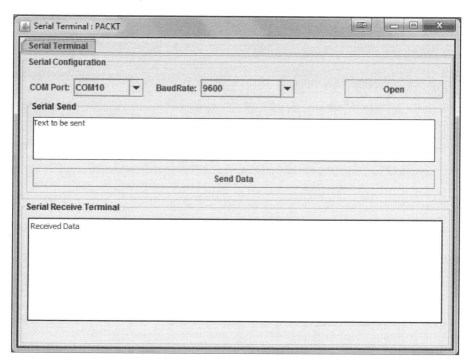

15. You can click on **Open** after you have selected the right COM port. You can interact with the serial terminal by sending a message to it and you will see that it works like Arduino IDE's serial monitor. A screenshot of this process can be found here:

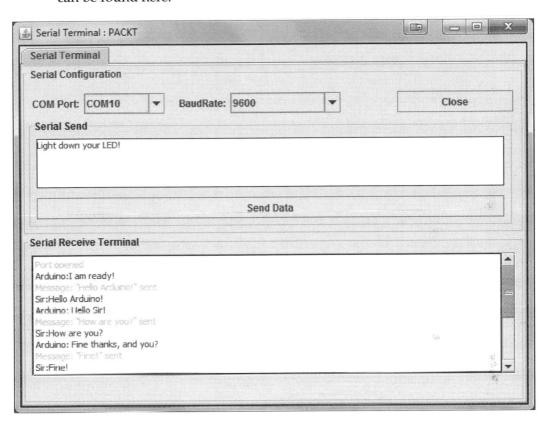

An explanation of the code can be found in the README file which is available from GitHub. So, let's navigate to an important line in the `SerialComm.java` file. In the `SerialEvent` function, there is a commented line, as shown here:

```
//ProcessMessage(receivedMsg);
```

If you uncomment this line and implement your own `ProcessMessage(String msg)` function, you can do custom stuff when you receive a message. For example, when Arduino sends you the `Hello Sir!` message, you can start an OpenCV application. This simple `ProcessMessage` function is implemented as shown here:

```
private void ProcessMessage(String msg)
  {
    if(msg.matches("(.*)Hello Sir!(.*)") == true)
    {
```

```
String cmd = "C:\\opencv_app.exe";
    Process p;
try {
  p = Runtime.getRuntime().exec(cmd);
  p.waitFor();
} catch (IOException e) {
  e.printStackTrace();
} catch (InterruptedException e) {
  e.printStackTrace();
}

  }
}
```

This function runs the executable application opencv_app.exe located under C:\ when it receives the Hello Sir! message from the serial port.

Normally, it is better to exchange data with a communication protocol instead of with normal language sentences. This will reduce the *overhead* to transfer the information. In our application, we have used the sentence Light up your LED! to light up an LED on Arduino. Normally, this task is achieved with a much shorter command, L1!. To light down the LED, the L0! command is used. Both cases are examples of string-based communication. To reduce the data overhead, it is possible to use binary protocols. It is hard to understand the content of a binary protocol message with the human eye but it is more efficient in terms of transfer data overhead. This will be handled in the last chapter. So, try to understand the communication capabilities of Arduino and Java and practice more and more!

Communicating with C++

It is also possible to connect the Arduino to your vision controller by using C++. In this case, it is a must to use platform libraries to communicate with the serial port drivers of the operating system.

If you use the OpenCV C++ API, it is best to implement the communication software in C++ even if communication is platform-dependent. Such architecture will simplify the communication scheme and it will enable you to combine communication capabilities with vision capabilities directly. We'll look at this communication scheme in the last chapter but not too deeply here.

 To get an insight of serial communication with Windows using C++, you can visit the Arduino documentation page at http://playground. arduino.cc/Interfacing/CPPWindows.

Summary

In this chapter you have learned how to use Arduino communication in an effective and efficient way. Additionally, you have learned how to establish a serial connection between the Arduino and the vision controller application. You also learned hardware-independent communication techniques for both wireless and wired communication. Data transfer is also a crucial part of robotics so please practice as much as possible and get ready for the next chapter!

In the next chapter, you will touch the physical world by using Arduino!

8
Acting in the Real World with Arduino

In previous chapters, you learned how to build the sub-blocks of a computer vision system. You've also learned how to use the Arduino as a sensor data collector and how to establish communication between the Arduino and the vision controller. With all this knowledge, it is possible to design a computer vision system which can make high-level conclusions from complex scenes. Up until now, the missing link was proceeding to the correct action following the vision system conclusion. This is what this chapter will show you! We'll also use the knowledge we gain here in the subsequent chapter.

In this chapter, you will learn about the most common embedded systems tools which interact with the physical world. Controlling motors and driving display screens are two of the most frequent implementations that display the output of the vision system to the real world. This chapter will teach you how to link motors and displays. In this process, you will build a solid foundation to control the motors in a robot or display various kinds of information on LCD or TFT displays.

Interfacing electric motors

Electric motors are the *motion providers* of electromechanical systems. They simply convert electrical energy into motion. Since we'll be dealing with electric motors in our design, we'll use the term *motor* for electric motor.

Motors are widely used in everyday life. Hairdryers, washing machines, fans, printers, and robots are some well-known examples that use electric motors. Using motors gives us the power to automate systems that touch the physical world. Moreover, the success of all these motion-enabled products is dependent on the control of the motion. This section aims to give you the ability to make efficient use of different kinds of motors.

In terms of their usage, electrical motors seem very simple. Connect the terminals of a motor to a battery with enough power, and the shaft will spin! But what if we want to spin the motor in the opposite direction? Connecting the wires in reverse order is one choice. Let's ask another question: what should we do if we want to spin the motor at quarter speed? The proper usage of a motor requires some knowledge. There are three major types of electric motors which we will introduce in this chapter. To make our job easier and focus on robotics applications, we will introduce a motor control shield. It can be used for driving various kinds of motors.

A good motor controller shield can be found on the Arduino website at `http://www.arduino.cc/en/Main/ArduinoMotorShieldR3`.

Driving DC motors

The first motor type to be introduced is the **Direct Current** (**DC**) motor. DC motors are the source of locomotion for moving robots. They are connected to the wheel of a sumo robot or the propeller of a quadrocopter. DC motors are generally used for transportation purposes. For land robotics applications, DC motors are used with a gear head to increase the torque needed. This operation will decrease the speed and vice versa. The following picture shows a typical DC motor with an in-built gear system:

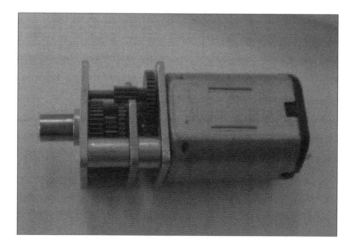

A DC motor has two pins. These two pins are used for both the power supply and the motion control. Do not forget that a motor will consume a lot of electrical energy when in motion. When the motor is spinning, it requires much more current than the Arduino can safely provide. You cannot connect the DC motor directly to the Arduino because the current consumption will be more than the maximum current value which the Arduino can provide over a pin,. The solution is a motor driver IC such as the L293D or L298D. These driver IC's take the motion control input from the Arduino and the required power from an external power source. By using the driver IC's, it becomes possible to drive the motors safely.

The speed of the motor is proportional to the power applied to it, and power is the product of voltage and current. The power is the multiplication of voltage by current. In digital systems, voltage levels are digital, so you have either zero or a constant value. On the Arduino, a high level pin voltage is 3.3V or 5V for some boards. For the Arduino Uno, it is 5V.

To be able to control the power provided by the pin it is necessary to switch the pin from time to time. This kind of modulation is called **Pulse Width Modulation (PWM)** and it is the basic tool of the electrical control. As the result of the PWM control, square waves are produced and the duty cycle of the square waves directly affects the power.

If you give 5V directly to a motor rated for 5V, it will run at maximum speed and consume maximum power. Imagine that you applied 0V to the motor for 5 ms and 5V for 5 ms, and so on. In this process the PWM's duty cycle is 50 percent because, in one period, the pin is at a high voltage for 50 percent of the time. If the motor is on for 50 percent of the time throughout each cycle, and has no load, that gives a 50 percent duty cycle, which will result in 50 percent of the rated no-load speed of the motor. If it is on for 10 percent of the time instead, during the same cycle, that gives a 10 percent duty cycle and roughly 10 percent of the speed. It should be noted that a 50 percent duty cycle may not perfectly correspond to 50 percent of the speed. In a 10 ms period, if you apply PWM with a 10 percent duty cycle it means that for only 1 ms of the total period will the pin stay on high voltage, and for the rest of the period the pin will stay on low level voltage.

In this case you expect that the motor will run at 10 percent of its maximum speed. Here, in the following diagram, you can see the different PWM's for a period of 20 ms:

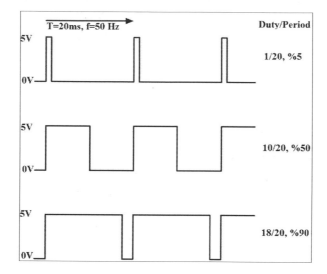

The period (or frequency) of the PWM signal is also very important. If you select a period of 10 seconds, the motion of the motor will not be continuous; it will start and stop, and so on. If you select the period low enough (for example 20 ms),the motion of the motor will be continuous. This is partly because the momentum of the motor will be enough to carry it through the *off* periods.

Another important point is that, if you select the duty rate of the PWM to be too low, the motor will consume energy but not move. The energy won't be sufficient to get over the motor's inertia. In other words, the energy won't be sufficient to run the motor.

PWM is used for many applications and the working principal is the same for other electro-physical convertors. If you apply 50 percent PWM to an LED, you will get a brightness of half of the maximum. Similarly, if you apply 25 percent PWM to a buzzer, the sound level will be a quarter of the maximum.

Another important topic is the direction management of the DC motor. Assume that you have named the pins of the motor A and B. When you connect the A pin to high and the B pin to low, the motor goes forward. In other words, the motor will go backwards if you connect the A pin to low and the B pin to high. Connecting two pins of the motor to the same logical level will create a brake effect.

> To be able to drive a pin to high or low in Arduino, you should use the function `digitalWrite(pin, value)`. This function is very well documented at http://www.arduino.cc/en/Reference/DigitalWrite.
>
> Similarly, to drive a pin with PWM you should use the function `analogWrite(pin, value)`. Here, the value property cannot be greater than 255. So, 255 is for nearly 100 percent PWM's and 128 can be used for 50 percent PWM's. The function is very well documented at http://www.arduino.cc/en/Reference/analogWrite. Also, please keep in mind that only certain Arduino pins are capable of PWM.

Driving stepper motors

Stepper motors are a little bit different to regular DC motors. Stepper motors are designed to spin in accurate increments. These motors move increment-by-increment or step-by-step. In other words, their rotations are the sum of their exact steps. For example, think about 3D printers that need precision instead of high **rotations per minute (rpm)**. Some applications require precision instead of speed, such as the back-and-forth operations of printers. Stepper motors then become very important.

We are about to cover a comprehensive example that will help us to understand how to drive a stepper motor using a controller. We will control a stepper motor using a potentiometer knob. In this example, we use the potentiometer knob as the control input. The rotation of the knob makes the stepper motor turn in the same direction as the knob. We will also learn how to construct a circuit to drive a stepper motor. In this particular circuit we will use the L293D motor driver IC, a 10K potentiometer, a breadboard, and a bunch of jumper cables. After covering this example you will have enough knowledge to implement a stepper motor in a project where precision is needed.

The application example in the Arduino documentation explains the concept very well. Because of this, we'll go through it here. Refer to the following diagram for the construction of the circuit:

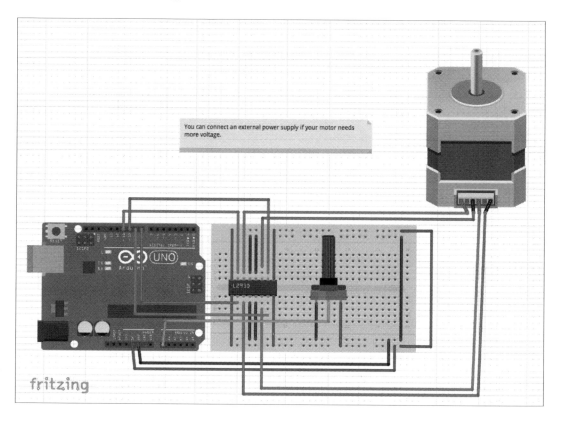

Here is the code:

```
/*
 * MotorKnob
 *
 * A stepper motor follows the turns of a potentiometer
 * (or other sensor) on analog input 0.
 *
 * http://www.arduino.cc/en/Reference/Stepper
 * This example code is in the public domain.
 */

#include <Stepper.h>
```

```
// change this to the number of steps on your motor
#define STEPS 100

// create an instance of the stepper class, specifying
// the number of steps of the motor and the pins it's
// attached to
Stepper stepper(STEPS, 8, 9, 10, 11);

// the previous reading from the analog input
int previous = 0;

void setup()
{
  // set the speed of the motor to 30 RPMs
  stepper.setSpeed(30);
}

void loop()
{
  // get the sensor value
  int val = analogRead(0);

  // move a number of steps equal to the change in the
  // sensor reading
  stepper.step(val - previous);

  // remember the previous value of the sensor
  previous = val;
}
```

We can now move on to an explanation of the code! Let's start explaining these lines first:

```
#include <Stepper.h>
#define STEPS 100
Stepper stepper(STEPS, 8, 9, 10, 11);
int previous = 0;
```

The STEPS property defines the number of steps required for one revolution of the stepper motor. Stepper motors have a resolution that corresponds to the minimum amount of angle step required so that they can turn. To calculate the STEPS property, you need to divide the minimum step of your stepper motor by 360 degrees or 360 degrees per resolution of the motor. Another common value for the STEPS property is 200 steps per revolution. The resolution of the motor can be seen in its datasheet.

An instance of the `stepper` class is created with the required parameters in the `stepper(STEPS, 8, 9, 10, 11)` method, where `STEPS, 8, 9, 10, 11` corresponds to the step resolution and the required pins. Then, the `previous` variable is initiated with the value `0`. This variable is used in the subtraction operation indicating both the magnitude of the next movement and the direction of the movement. You can set the stepper speed as shown here:

```
void setup()
{
  stepper.setSpeed(30);
}
```

In the `setup` function, we set the speed of the stepper motor by declaring the rotation per minute value to the `stepper.setSpeed` method. In this case, we set the rpm to `30`.

Here is the remaining code:

```
void loop()
{
  int val = analogRead(0);
  stepper.step(val - previous);
  previous = val;
}
```

In the `loop` function we read the analog 0 pin and put it into the `val` variable. It will be necessary while stepping the motor. Then, the `val - previous` subtraction in the `steper.step` method gives an amount and direction for the `step` method. Any non-zero value can be seen as a movement on the stepper motor. After calling the `step(val-previous)` method, the motor will settle into the new position. Lastly, for the next computation, we set the `previous` value to the `val` variable to use it in the next cycle.

Driving servo motors

Servo motors were originally designed to rotate a fixed range of angles, often between 0 to 180 degrees. So, originally they could not spin continuously. Although it is possible to hack servo motors and make them continuous, we won't separately handle standard and continuous servos owing to the fact that the principals of the operations are the same. Servo motors are widely used in robotics and they are probably the best option for highly precise small movements which need high torque. The major advantage of servo motors is that they include the controller circuit inside. This means that you don't need an external circuit or shield to drive and control a small servo motor.

We will cover an example for driving a servo with the Arduino. For now, the required connection for one servo motor is shown in the following circuit diagram. Do not forget that, if you need more power or a higher voltage level, you can connect the power pins of the servo motor to an external power source:

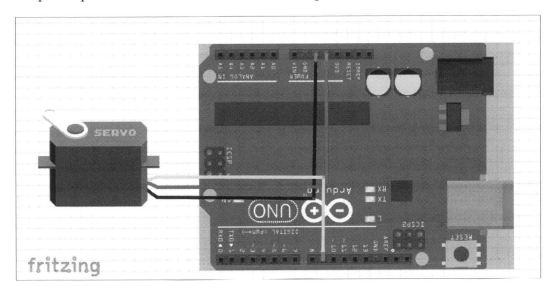

Here is the complete servo code:

```
#include <Servo.h>
Servo myservo;
int pos = 0;
void setup()
{
  myservo.attach(9);
}

void loop()
{
  for(pos = 0; pos < 180; pos++)
  {
    myservo.write(pos);
    delay(15);
  }
  for(pos = 180; pos>=1; pos--)
  {
    myservo.write(pos);
    delay(15);
  }
}
```

Let's go through the servo example code and understand the process required to control the servo:

```
#include <Servo.h>
Servo myservo;
int pos = 0;
void setup()
{
  myservo.attach(9);
}
```

As always, we include the required header files. In this case, we add the `Servo.h` header file. The next step is to create our servo object, `myservo`. Then we set the neutral position of the servo as `pos = 0`. After that, we initiate the `myservo` object by attaching pin `9`. Do not forget that the pin must be capable of PWM. Here is the looping code:

```
void loop()
{
  for(pos = 0; pos < 180; pos++)
  {
    myservo.write(pos);
    delay(15);
  }
  for(pos = 180; pos>=1; pos--)
  {
    myservo.write(pos);
    delay(15);
  }
}
```

The code in the `loop` function basically sweeps from 0 to 180 and returns to 0 again. Let's look at this code in more detail. First, the `for` loop starts from position 0 and increments the next position of the `myservo` object by assigning a new position with the `write` method. Since running a `for` loop is much faster than the movement of the servo, the code has a `delay` function, with a value of 15 micro seconds, to give enough time for the servo to reach the next position before its next updated position. Similarly, the second `for` loop decrements the current position of the servo one by one from 180 to 0.

Using display screens

Some computer vision applications are ended with information transfer. One of the best ways of making information transfer from embedded systems to a human is by using display screens. In addition to the conclusion of the vision controller, it is possible to give extra information about the environment or the system by using display screens. It is always an alternative to sending the information to a mobile phone or computer instead of displaying it on a dedicated display screen. On the other hand, using a local display simply makes everything easier and creates a better user experience in some cases. The following are examples of display screens.

There are many types of display screens but the main ones are **Liquid Crystal Display (LCD)** and **thin-film transistor (TFT)** screens. LCD screens are simple and cheap devices which can be used for mono-color display operations. TFT screens are more powerful devices for displaying richer screens with multi-color shapes and texts. TFT screens can also be integrated with touch interfaces which enable the user to directly interact with the screen and the system. In this section, we will introduce how to use these display screens properly but we won't discuss the touch and the user interface design because they are out of the scope of this book.

Using LCD screens

Liquid Crystal Displays (LCD) are one of the most widely used display interfaces in Arduino applications. LCD screens are really easy to use. They are also cheaper than full color TFT screens. They are very good for displaying menus, sensor readings and the system status. We will introduce an example of a generic LCD display that has a Hitachi HD44780 driver. You will need a breadboard, one 10 K potentiometer, a HD44780 compatible LCD display and jumper wires. In the following diagram, you can see the required connections:

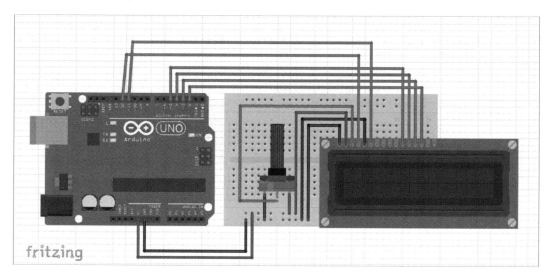

You can find an example of the LCD driver code on the Arduino website, which is also given here. Because it explains the concepts very well and is also easy to modify, we'll go through it:

```
/*
  LiquidCrystal Library - Hello World

Demonstrates the use a 16x2 LCD display. The LiquidCrystal
library works with all LCD displays that are compatible with the
Hitachi HD44780 driver. There are many of them out there, and you
can usually tell them by the 16-pin interface.

This sketch prints "Hello World!" to the LCD
and shows the time.

 The circuit:
* LCD RS pin to digital pin 12
* LCD Enable pin to digital pin 11
```

```
* LCD D4 pin to digital pin 5
* LCD D5 pin to digital pin 4
* LCD D6 pin to digital pin 3
* LCD D7 pin to digital pin 2
* LCD R/W pin to ground
* 10K resistor:
* ends to +5V and ground
* wiper to LCD VO pin (pin 3)

Library originally added 18 Apr 2008
by David A. Mellis
library modified 5 Jul 2009
by Limor Fried (http://www.ladyada.net)
example added 9 Jul 2009
by Tom Igoe
modified 22 Nov 2010
by Tom Igoe

This example code is in the public domain.

http://www.arduino.cc/en/Tutorial/LiquidCrystal
*/

// include the library code:
#include <LiquidCrystal.h>

// initialize the library with the numbers of the interface pins
LiquidCrystal lcd(12, 11, 5, 4, 3, 2);

void setup() {
  // set up the LCD's number of columns and rows:
  lcd.begin(16, 2);
  // Print a message to the LCD.
  lcd.print("hello, world!");
}

void loop() {
  // set the cursor to column 0, line 1
  // (note: line 1 is the second row, since counting begins with
0):
  lcd.setCursor(0, 1);
  // print the number of seconds since reset:
  lcd.print(millis()/1000);
}
```

Let's explain the code:

```
#include <LiquidCrystal.h>
```

As usual, the header file for the liquid crystal is added. After that, the instance is created with the `LiquidCrystal lcd(12, 11, 5, 4, 3, 2)` call. Here is the remaining code:

```
void setup() {
  lcd.begin(16, 2);
  lcd.print("hello, world!");
}
```

Initialization is done by `lcd.begin(16, 2)` with values of `16` and `2`, which correspond to the number of columns and rows. Then the `hello, world!` message is printed to a screen. Here is the remaining code:

```
void loop() {
  lcd.setCursor(0, 1);
  lcd.print(millis()/1000);
}
```

In the `loop` function, the starting point of print is set by `lcd.setCursor(0, 1)` statement. Lastly, the `lcd.print(millis()/1000)` statement prints one in a thousand milliseconds from the Arduino after it was started.

Using TFT screens

TFT screens are much more visually rich than the LCD screens we introduced earlier. It is possible to display graphic user interfaces by using TFT screens and the sky is the limit for graphic interface design. TFT screens are not only good for displaying stationary images, they are also capable of displaying rich animations. The major disadvantage of TFT screens are their price.

In this section, we'll talk about how to use TFT in a simple manner. The Arduino website has a very good and rich documentation on the advanced usage of the TFT screen. So, please follow the relevant link to get more information.

 For more information on the Arduino TFT screen, visit the product page at http://www.arduino.cc/en/Main/GTFT.

Graphic design is a kind of art, so it cannot be modeled easily. We won't handle visual design and user interaction here because they are big subjects and not within the scope of this book. On the other hand, improving your artistic capabilities will make your products and applications much more professional and popular. The following picture shows you a typical screen that can be used along with the Arduino:

Here is the code for the Arduino TFT example:

```
/*
  Arduino TFT text example

  This example demonstrates how to draw text on the
  TFT with an Arduino. The Arduino reads the value
  of an analog sensor attached to pin A0, and writes
  the value to the LCD screen, updating every
  quarter second.

  This example code is in the public domain

  Created 15 April 2013 by Scott Fitzgerald

  http://www.arduino.cc/en/Tutorial/TFTDisplayText

*/

#include <TFT.h> // Arduino LCD library
#include <SPI.h>
```

```
// pin definition for the Uno
#define cs    10
#define dc    9
#define rst   8

// pin definition for the Leonardo
// #define cs    7
// #define dc    0
// #define rst   1

// create an instance of the library
TFT TFTscreen = TFT(cs, dc, rst);

// char array to print to the screen
char sensorPrintout[4];

void setup() {

  // Put this line at the beginning of every sketch that uses the
GLCD:
  TFTscreen.begin();

  // clear the screen with a black background
  TFTscreen.background(0, 0, 0);

  // write the static text to the screen
  // set the font color to white
  TFTscreen.stroke(255, 255, 255);
  // set the font size
  TFTscreen.setTextSize(2);
  // write the text to the top left corner of the screen
  TFTscreen.text("Sensor Value :\n ", 0, 0);
  // ste the font size very large for the loop
  TFTscreen.setTextSize(5);
}

void loop() {

  // Read the value of the sensor on A0
  String sensorVal = String(analogRead(A0));

  // convert the reading to a char array
  sensorVal.toCharArray(sensorPrintout, 4);
```

```
  // set the font color
  TFTscreen.stroke(255, 255, 255);
  // print the sensor value
  TFTscreen.text(sensorPrintout, 0, 20);
  // wait for a moment
  delay(250);
  // erase the text you just wrote
  TFTscreen.stroke(0, 0, 0);
  TFTscreen.text(sensorPrintout, 0, 20);
}
```

Let's explain the code:

```
#include <TFT.h>
#include <SPI.h>

// pin definition for the Uno
#define cs    10
#define dc    9
#define rst   8

TFT TFTscreen = TFT(cs, dc, rst);

char sensorPrintout[4];
```

We need to add both the TFT.h file and the SPI.h file to call the necessary functions. In addition to the TFT header file, we need to add the SPI header file because the Arduino and the TFT screen communicate through the SPI protocol. The required pins for SPI communication are defined. After, we create our instance TFT TFTscreen = TFT(cs, dc, rst) by initiating the object with the required SPI pin definitions. Next, it is time to create a character string array sensorPrintout[4] to store the Printout information to display on the screen. Here is the remaining code:

```
void setup() {
  TFTscreen.begin();
  TFTscreen.background(0, 0, 0);
  TFTscreen.stroke(255, 255, 255);
  TFTscreen.setTextSize(2);
  TFTscreen.text("Sensor Value :\n ", 0, 0);
  TFTscreen.setTextSize(5);
}
```

We initiate the object by calling the TFTscreen.begin method. After that, we set the background color to black with the TFTscreen.background(0, 0, 0) call. Additionally, the font color is set to white by the TFTscreen.stroke(255,255,255) call. Note that, in RGB color space maximum values, 255, of all three colors give white and minimum values, 0, gives a black color.

Next, TFTscreen.setTextSize(2) sets the size of the fonts. The TFTscreen. text method anchors the Sensor Value : to the top left. Lastly, the TFTscreen. setTextSize(5) method is called to make the sensor value bigger than the text. Here is the remaining code:

```
void loop() {
    String sensorVal = String(analogRead(A0));
    sensorVal.toCharArray(sensorPrintout, 4);
    TFTscreen.stroke(255, 255, 255);
    TFTscreen.text(sensorPrintout, 0, 20);
    delay(250);
    TFTscreen.stroke(0, 0, 0);
    TFTscreen.text(sensorPrintout, 0, 20);
}
```

In the loop function, the value of the analog pin 0 is stored in the string object sensorVal. Next, the sensorVal string is parsed in to individual characters. For example, the 1234 string is converted into 1, 2, 3, and 4. This is done to make sure that we always have an array of four characters. Next, the font color setting is done by the TFTscreen.stroke(255, 255, 255) method to make it a white color. Then, the character array is given to the screen by the text method with the starting coordinates on the screen. A delay function delay(250) puts a quarter of a second delay and deletion of the text is applied by the TFTscreen.stroke(0, 0, 0) call and re-written to the screen by the text method.

Summary

Let's now summarize what we learned in this chapter. What we've built in this chapter is an interaction with physical life by using the Arduino. Now you are capable of converting the conclusions of the vision controller to a real physical act! Of course, performing the correct actions across the board is crucial. This chapter gave you the best practices to enable you to produce the best design for your own application's needs.

Now, it is time to combine everything you've learned from this book and build it into real life examples. In the next chapter you will learn how to combine everything you have learned up till now and how to build a complex system easily. Get ready for the next chapter!

9

Building a "Click-to-Go" Robot

Up until now, you have gained background on how to approach computer vision applications, how to divide an application development process into basic steps, how to realize these design steps and how to combine a vision system with the Arduino. Now it is time to connect all the pieces into one!

In this chapter you will learn about building a vision-assisted robot which can go to any point you want within the boundaries of the camera's sight. In this scenario there will be a camera attached to the ceiling and, once you get the video stream from the robot and click on any place in the view, the robot will go there. This application will combine all the chapters and will give you an all-in-one development application. You will see that you can use the approach in this book for any kind of Arduino vision project!

System overview

Before getting started, let's try to draw the application scheme and define the potential steps. We want to build a vision-enabled robot which can be controlled via a camera attached to the ceiling and, when we click on any point in the camera view, we want our robot to go to this specific point.

This operation requires a mobile robot that can communicate with the vision system. The vision system should be able to detect or recognize the robot and calculate the position and orientation of the robot. The vision system should also give us the opportunity to click on any point in the view and it should calculate the path and the robot movements to get to the destination. This scheme requires a communication line between the robot and the vision controller. In the following illustration, you can see the physical scheme of the application setup on the left hand side and the user application window on the right hand side:

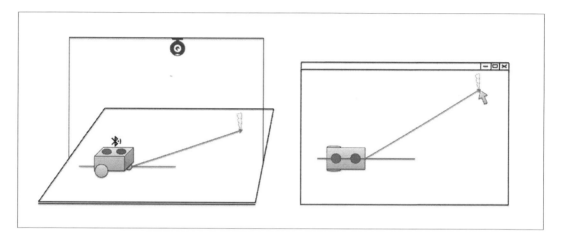

After interpreting the application scheme, the next step is to divide the application into small steps by using the computer vision approach, which was presented in *Chapter 1, General Overview of Computer Vision Systems*, and explained in the following chapters.

In the data acquisition phase, we'll only use the scene's video stream. There won't be an external sensor on the robot because, for this application, we don't need one. Camera selection is important and the camera distance (the height from the robot plane) should be enough to see the whole area. We'll use the blue and red circles above the robot to detect the robot and calculate its orientation. We don't need smaller details. A resolution of about 640x480 pixels is sufficient for a camera distance of 120 cm. We need an RGB camera stream because we'll use the color properties of the circles. We will use the Logitech C110, which is an affordable webcam. Any other OpenCV compatible webcam will work because this application is not very demanding in terms of vision input. If you need more cable length you can use a USB extension cable.

In the preprocessing phase, the first step is to remove the small details from the surface. Blurring is a simple and effective operation for this purpose. If you need to, you can resize your input image to reduce the image size and processing time. Do not forget that, if you resize to too small a resolution, you won't be able to extract useful information. The following picture is of the Logitech C110 webcam:

The next step is processing. There are two main steps in this phase. The first step is to detect the circles in the image. The second step is to calculate the robot orientation and the path to the destination point. The robot can then follow the path and reach its destination. In *Chapter 5*, *Processing Vision Data with OpenCV*, we discussed color processing with which we can apply color filters to the image to get the image masks of the red circle and the blue circle, as shown in the following picture. Then we can use contour detection or blob analysis to detect the circles and extract useful features. It is important to keep it simple and logical:

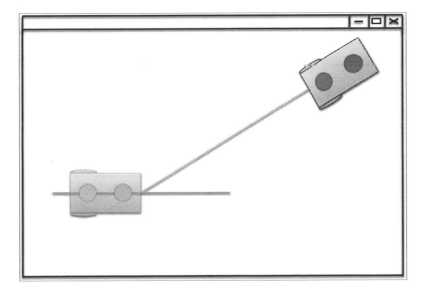

Blob analysis detects the bounding boxes of two circles on the robot and, if we draw a line between the centers of the circles, once we calculate the line angle, we will get the orientation of the robot itself. The mid-point of this line will be the center of the robot. If we draw a line from the center of the robot to the destination point we obtain the straightest route. The circles on the robot can also be detected by using the Hough transform for circles but, because it is a relatively slow algorithm and it is hard to extract image statistics from the results, the blob analysis-based approach is better.

Another approach is by using the SURF, SIFT or ORB features as discussed in *Chapter 5, Processing Vision Data with OpenCV*. But these methods probably won't provide fast real-time behavior, so blob analysis will probably work better.

After detecting blobs, we can apply post-filtering to remove the unwanted blobs. We can use the diameter of the circles, the area of the bounding box, and the color information, to filter the unwanted blobs.

By using the properties of the blobs (extracted features), it is possible to detect or recognize the circles, and then the robot. To be able to check if the robot has reached the destination or not, a distance calculation from the center of the robot to the destination point would be useful. In this scenario, the robot will be detected by our vision controller. Detecting the center of the robot is sufficient to track the robot.

Once we calculate the robot's position and orientation, we can combine this information with the distance and orientation to the destination point and we can send the robot the commands to move it! Efficient planning algorithms can be applied in this phase but, because it is not the focus of this book, we'll implement a simple path planning approach. Firstly, the robot will orientate itself towards the destination point by turning right or left and then it will go forward to reach the destination. This scenario will work for scenarios without obstacles. If you want to extend the application for a complex environment with obstacles, you should implement an obstacle detection mechanism and an efficient path planning algorithm.

We can send the commands such as `Left!`, `Right!`, `Go!`, or `Stop!` to the robot over a wireless line. RF communication is an efficient solution for this problem. In this scenario, we need two NRF24L01 modules—the first module is connected to the robot controller and the other is connected to the vision controller.

The Arduino is the perfect means to control the robot and communicate with the vision controller. The vision controller can be built on any hardware platform such as a PC, tablet, or a smartphone. The vision controller application can be implemented on lots of operating systems as OpenCV is platform-independent. We preferred Windows and a laptop to run our vision controller application.

As you can see, we have divided our application into small and easy-to-implement parts, as recommended in previous chapters. Now it is time to build them all!

Building a robot

It is time to explain how to build our Click-to-Go robot. Before going any further we would like to boldly say that robotic projects can teach us the fundamental fields of science such as mechanics, electronics, and programming. We will cover these topics in the following sections of this chapter.

As we go through the building process of our Click-to-Go robot, you will see that we have kept it as simple as possible. Moreover, instead of buying ready-to-use robot kits, we have built our own simple and robust robot. Of course, if you are planning to buy a robot kit or already have a kit available, you can simply adapt your existing robot into this project.

Our robot design is relatively simple in terms of mechanics. We will use only a box-shaped container platform, two gear motors with two individual wheels, a battery to drive the motors, one nRF24L01 **Radio Frequency (RF)** transceiver module, a bunch of jumper wires, an L293D IC and, of course, one Arduino Uno board module. We will use one more nRF24L01 and one more Arduino Uno for the vision controller communication circuit.

Our Click-to-Go robot will be operated by a simplified version of a differential drive. A differential drive can be summarized as a relative speed change on the wheels, which assigns a direction to the robot. In other words, if both wheels spin at the same rate, the robot goes forward. To drive in reverse, the wheels spin in the opposite direction. To turn left, the left wheel turns backwards and the right wheel stays still or turns forwards. Similarly, to turn right, the right wheel turns backwards and the left stays still or turns forwards.

You can get curved paths by varying the rotation speeds of the wheels. Yet, to cover every aspect of this comprehensive project, we will drive the wheels of both the motors forward to go forwards. To turn left, the left wheel stays still and the right wheel turns forward. Symmetrically, to turn right, the right motor stays still and the left motor runs forward. We will not use running motors in a reverse direction to go backwards. Instead, we will change the direction of the robot by turning right or left.

Building mechanics

As we stated earlier, the mechanics of the robot are fairly simple. First of all we need a small box-shaped container to use as both a rigid surface and the storage for the battery and electronics. For this purpose, we will use a simple plywood box. We will attach gear motors in front of the plywood box and any kind of support surface to the bottom of the box. As can be seen in the following picture, we used a small wooden rod to support the back of the robot to level the box:

 If you think that the wooden rod support is dragging, we recommend adding a small ball support similar to Pololu's ball caster, shown at https://www.pololu.com/product/950. It is not a very expensive component and it significantly improves the mobility of the robot.

You may want to drill two holes next to the motor wirings to keep the platform tidy. The easiest way to attach the motors and the support rod is by using two-sided tape. Just make sure that the tape is not too thin. It is much better to use two-sided foamy tape.

The topside of the robot can be covered with a black shell to enhance the contrast between the red and blue circles. We will use these circles to ascertain the orientation of the robot during the operation, as mentioned earlier. For now, don't worry too much about this detail. Just be aware that we need to cover the top of the robot with a flat surface. We will explain in detail in the latter part of the chapter how these red and blue circles are used. It is worth mentioning that we used large water bottle lids. It is better to use matt surfaces instead of shiny surfaces to avoid glare in the image.

The finished Click-to-Go robot should be similar to the robot shown in the following picture. The robot's head is on the side with the red circle:

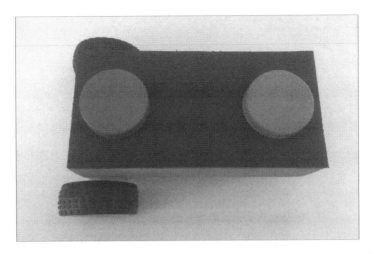

As we have now covered building the mechanics of our robot we can move on to building the electronics.

Building the electronics

We will use two separate Arduino Unos for this vision-enabled robot project, one each for the robot and the transmitter system. The electronic setup needs a little bit more attention than the mechanics. The electronic components of the robot and the transmitter units are similar. However, the robot needs more work.

We have selected nRF24L01 modules for the wireless communication module,. These modules are reliable and easy to find from both the Internet and local hobby stores. It is possible to use any pair of wireless connectivity modules but, for this project, we will stick with nRF24L01 modules, as shown in this picture:

For the driving motors we will need to use a quadruple half-H driver, L293D. Again, every electronic shop should have these ICs. As a reminder, you may need to buy a couple of spare L293D ICs in case you burn the IC by mistake. Following is the picture of the L293D IC:

We will need a bunch of jumper wires to connect the components together. It is nice to have a small breadboard for the robot/receiver, to wire the L293D. The transmitter part is very simple so a breadboard is not essential.

Robot/receiver and transmitter drawings

The drawings of both the receiver and the transmitter have two common modules: Arduino Uno and nRF24L01 connectivity modules. The connections of the nRF24L01 modules on both sides are the same. In addition to these connectivity modules, for the receiver, we need to put some effort into connecting the L293D IC and the battery to power up the motors.

In the following picture, we can see a drawing of the transmitter. As it will always be connected to the OpenCV platform via the USB cable, there is no need to feed the system with an external battery:

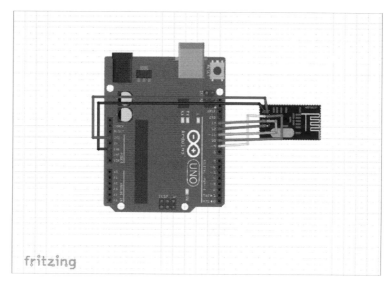

As shown in the following picture of the receiver and the robot, it is a good idea to separate the motor battery from the battery that feeds the Arduino Uno board because the motors may draw high loads or create high loads, which can easily damage the Arduino board's pin outs. Another reason is to keep the Arduino working even if the battery motor has drained. Separating the feeder batteries is a very good practice to follow if you are planning to use more than one 12V battery. To keep everything safe, we fed the Arduino Uno with a 6V battery pack and the motors with a 9V battery:

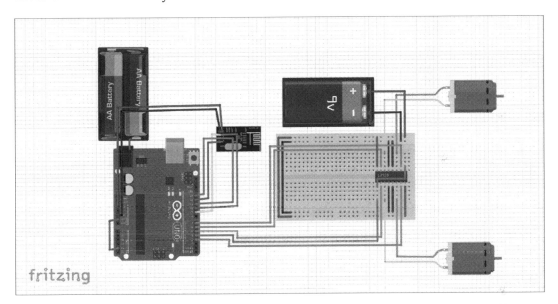

 Drawings of receiver systems can be little bit confusing and lead to errors. It is a good idea to open the drawings and investigate how the connections are made by using Fritzing. You can download the Fritzing drawings of this project from https://github.com/ozenozkaya/ click_to_go_robot_drawings.

To download the Fritzing application, visit the Fritzing download page:

http://fritzing.org/download/

Building the robot controller and communications

We are now ready to go through the software implementation of the robot and the transmitter. Basically what we are doing here is building the required connectivity to send data to the remote robot continuously from OpenCV via a transmitter. OpenCV will send commands to the transmitter through a USB cable to the first Arduino board, which will then send the data to the unit on the robot. And it will send this data to the remote robot over the RF module. Follow these steps:

1. Before explaining the code, we need to import the RF24 library. To download RF24 library drawings please go to the GitHub link at `https://github.com/maniacbug/RF24`.

2. After downloading the library, go to **Sketch | Include Library | Add .ZIP Library...** to include the library in the Arduino IDE environment.

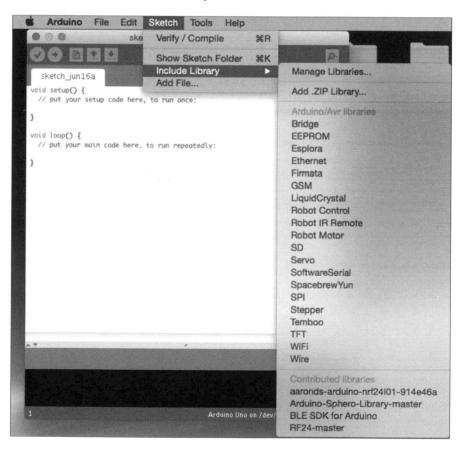

3. After clicking **Add .ZIP Library...**, a window will appear. Go into the **downloads** directory and select the **RF24-master** folder that you just downloaded. Now you are ready to use the RF24 library. As a reminder, it is pretty much the same to include a library in Arduino IDE as on other platforms. It is time to move on to the explanation of the code!

It is important to mention that we use the same code for both the robot and the transmitter, with a small trick! The same code works differently for the robot and the transmitter. Now, let's make everything simpler during the code explanation. The receiver mode needs to ground an analog 4 pin. The idea behind the operation is simple; we are setting the `role_pin` to high through its internal pull-up resistor. So, it will read high even if you don't connect it, but you can still safely connect it to ground and it will read low. Basically, the analog 4 pin reads 0 if the there is a connection with a ground pin. On the other hand, if there is no connection to the ground, the analog 4 pin value is kept as 1. By doing this at the beginning, we determine the role of the board and can use the same code on both sides. Here is the code:

 This example code is taken from one of the examples in the RF24 library. We have changed it in order to serve our needs in this project. The original example can be found in the `RF24-master/Examples/ pingpair` directory.

```
#include <SPI.h>
#include "nRF24L01.h"
#include "RF24.h"

#define MOTOR_PIN_1 3
#define MOTOR_PIN_2 5
#define MOTOR_PIN_3 6
#define MOTOR_PIN_4 7
#define ENABLE_PIN   4
#define SPI_ENABLE_PIN 9
#define SPI_SELECT_PIN 10

const int role_pin = A4;

typedef enum {transmitter = 1, receiver} e_role;

unsigned long motor_value[2];
```

```
String input_string = "";
boolean string_complete = false;

RF24 radio(SPI_ENABLE_PIN, SPI_SELECT_PIN);

const uint64_t pipes[2] = { 0xF0F0F0F0E1LL, 0xF0F0F0F0D2LL };

e_role role = receiver;

void setup() {
  pinMode(role_pin, INPUT);
  digitalWrite(role_pin, HIGH);
  delay(20);
  radio.begin();
  radio.setRetries(15, 15);
  Serial.begin(9600);
  Serial.println(" Setup Finished");
  if (digitalRead(role_pin)) {
    Serial.println(digitalRead(role_pin));
    role = transmitter;
  }
  else {
    Serial.println(digitalRead(role_pin));
    role = receiver;
  }

  if (role == transmitter) {

    radio.openWritingPipe(pipes[0]);
    radio.openReadingPipe(1, pipes[1]);
  }
  else {
    pinMode(MOTOR_PIN_1, OUTPUT);
    pinMode(MOTOR_PIN_2, OUTPUT);
    pinMode(MOTOR_PIN_3, OUTPUT);
    pinMode(MOTOR_PIN_4, OUTPUT);
    pinMode(ENABLE_PIN, OUTPUT);
    digitalWrite(ENABLE_PIN, HIGH);

    radio.openWritingPipe(pipes[1]);
    radio.openReadingPipe(1, pipes[0]);
  }
```

```
      radio.startListening();
}

void loop() {
// TRANSMITTER CODE BLOCK //
   if (role == transmitter) {
     Serial.println("Transmitter");
     if (string_complete)
     {
       if (input_string == "Right!")
       {
         motor_value[0] = 0;
         motor_value[1] = 120;
       }
       else if (input_string == "Left!")
       {
         motor_value[0] = 120;
         motor_value[1] = 0;
       }
       else if (input_string == "Go!")
       {
         motor_value[0] = 120;
         motor_value[1] = 110;
       }
       else
       {
         motor_value[0] = 0;
         motor_value[1] = 0;
       }
       input_string = "";
       string_complete = false;
     }

     radio.stopListening();
     radio.write(motor_value, 2 * sizeof(unsigned long));
     radio.startListening();
     delay(20);
   }
   // RECEIVER CODE BLOCK //
   if (role == receiver) {
     Serial.println("Receiver");
     if (radio.available()) {
```

```
        bool done = false;
        while (!done) {
          done = radio.read(motor_value, 2 * sizeof(unsigned long));
          delay(20);
        }

        Serial.println(motor_value[0]);
        Serial.println(motor_value[1]);
        analogWrite(MOTOR_PIN_1, motor_value[1]);
        digitalWrite(MOTOR_PIN_2, LOW);
        analogWrite(MOTOR_PIN_3, motor_value[0]);
        digitalWrite(MOTOR_PIN_4  , LOW);
        radio.stopListening();
        radio.startListening();
      }
    }
  }
void serialEvent() {
    while (Serial.available()) {
      // get the new byte:
      char inChar = (char)Serial.read();
      // add it to the inputString:
      input_string += inChar;
      // if the incoming character is a newline, set a flag
      // so the main loop can do something about it:
      if (inChar == '!' || inChar == '?') {
        string_complete = true;
        Serial.print("data_received");
      }
    }
  }
}
```

Let's start to explain the code starting from the very beginning:

```
#include <SPI.h>
#include "nRF24L01.h"
#include "RF24.h"

#define MOTOR_PIN_1 3
#define MOTOR_PIN_2 5
#define MOTOR_PIN_3 6
#define MOTOR_PIN_4 7
#define ENABLE_PIN  4
#define SPI_ENABLE_PIN 9
```

```
#define SPI_SELECT_PIN 10

const int role_pin = A4;
typedef enum {transmitter = 1, receiver} e_role;
unsigned long motor_value[2];
String input_string = "";
boolean string_complete = false;
RF24 radio(SPI_ENABLE_PIN, SPI_SELECT_PIN);
const uint64_t pipes[2] = { 0xF0F0F0F0E1LL, 0xF0F0F0F0D2LL };
e_role role = receiver;
```

We include required libraries such as SPI.h, nRF24L01.h, and RF24.h. Then we make a series of definitions about the motor pins and the SPI pins that we will use. After that the definition of the LED pin and the initiation of role_pin = A4 comes. The role_pin pin is the pin we were talking about before introducing the code that determines the role of the board. typedef enum is defined in order to store the possible roles of the board.

The serialEvent callback function-related variables are initiated, namely input_string and string_complete. The RF24 object radio is initiated by the SPI_ENABLE_PIN and SPI_SELECT_PIN pins.

The RF module-related communication pipe addresses are put into the pipes array. Then, the e_role role is set to receiver as default:

```
void setup() {
  pinMode(role_pin, INPUT);
  digitalWrite(role_pin, HIGH);
  delay(20);
  radio.begin();
  radio.setRetries(15, 15);
  Serial.begin(9600);
  Serial.println(" Setup Finished");
  if (digitalRead(role_pin)) {
    Serial.println(digitalRead(role_pin));
    role = transmitter;
  }
  else {
    Serial.println(digitalRead(role_pin));
    role = receiver;
  }

  if (role == transmitter) {
```

```
      radio.openWritingPipe(pipes[0]);
      radio.openReadingPipe(1, pipes[1]);
    }
    else {
      pinMode(MOTOR_PIN_1, OUTPUT);
      pinMode(MOTOR_PIN_2, OUTPUT);
      pinMode(MOTOR_PIN_3, OUTPUT);
      pinMode(MOTOR_PIN_4, OUTPUT);
      pinMode(ENABLE_PIN, OUTPUT);
      digitalWrite(ENABLE_PIN, HIGH);

      radio.openWritingPipe(pipes[1]);
      radio.openReadingPipe(1, pipes[0]);
    }

    radio.startListening();
  }
```

In the setup function, we start by determining the role of the board. The role_pin pin is therefore set to INPUT and to HIGH. Then a small delay function is placed just before the reading of role_pin. If role_pin is connected to ground, digitalRead(role_pin) returns 0. On the other hand, if the pin is not connected to the ground than we read 1. So, the role determination is made via the if else statement. Note that we use two separate Arduino Unos, one has a grounded role_pin, while the other one, the transmitter, has no grounding connection. In other words, the Arduino in the robot platform has grounding and the transmitter does not have the grounding of role_pin.

After this important role determination process, we call the Serial.begin and radio.begin methods to start the communication lines. Then, in the second if else statement, we set the writing and reading pipes of the transmitter and receiver roles. For the transmitter role we simply start reading and writing pipes. Similarly, for the receiver, we set the transmitter's writing pipes as the listening pipe of the receiver, and transmitter's reading pipe as the writing pipe of the receiver. This is similar to connecting two serial ports, RX and TX.

For the receiver role we need to set the motor control pins and ENABLE_PIN to OUTPUT. ENABLE_PIN feeds L293D enable pins which need to be fed by voltage (it is shown as orange wiring in the receiver drawings).

Lastly, the `radio.startListening` method is called to listen to any packet received. Here is the remaining code:

```
void loop() {
// TRANSMITTER CODE BLOCK //
 if (role == transmitter) {
  Serial.println("Transmitter");
  if (string_complete)
  {
   if (input_string == "Right!")
   {
    motor_value[0] = 0;
    motor_value[1] = 120;
   }
   else if (input_string == "Left!")
   {
    motor_value[0] = 120;
    motor_value[1] = 0;
   }
   else if (input_string == "Go!")
   {
    motor_value[0] = 120;
    motor_value[1] = 110;
   }
   else
   {
    motor_value[0] = 0;
    motor_value[1] = 0;
   }
   input_string = "";
   string_complete = false;
  }

  radio.stopListening();
  radio.write(motor_value, 2 * sizeof(unsigned long));
  radio.startListening();
  delay(20);
 }
// RECEIVER CODE BLOCK //
 if (role == receiver) {
  Serial.println("Receiver");
  if (radio.available()) {
```

```
   bool done = false;
   while (!done) {
    done = radio.read(motor_value, 2 * sizeof(unsigned long));
    delay(20);
   }

   Serial.println(motor_value[0]);
   Serial.println(motor_value[1]);
   analogWrite(MOTOR_PIN_1, motor_value[1]);
   digitalWrite(MOTOR_PIN_2, LOW);
   analogWrite(MOTOR_PIN_3, motor_value[0]);
   digitalWrite(MOTOR_PIN_4 , LOW);
   radio.stopListening();
   radio.startListening();
  }
 }
}
```

Before the explanation of the rest of the code, we would like to draw the mainframe of the loop function. In this function, there are two different code blocks, namely receiver and transmitter blocks. While the transmitter block takes sent commands from OpenCV via the USB cable and sends them to the receiver, the receiver code block takes commands from the transmitter. These commands are Go!, Left!, Right!, and Stop!. These direction commands remotely control our robot and navigate it to the desired location dynamically.

The transmitter block checks if a message has been received from OpenCV. This listening is done by the serialEvent function. The transmitter code block updates the motor drive motor_value[0] and motor_value[1] values to keep the robot in control according to the incoming commands from OpenCV. After listening each time, it is necessary to flush the read data from input_string, and string_complete needs to be set to false.

Data transmission to the receiver is made by a sequence of RF24 library methods. Firstly, the radio.stopListening method sets the chip select pin to LOW and flushes the RX and TX buffers. After that, the radio.Write method sends the motor_value array data to the receiver and waits for the acknowledgement from the receiver. Then, the radio.startListening methods pull up the chip select pin to HIGH for the listening receiver.

In the receiver code block, if(radio.available()) is satisfied and the radio. read method listens to the incoming data which is sent by the transmitter. When the transmitted data is finished, the radio.read method returns true and sets the done variable to true. Then the code exits from the while(! done) loop and sends appropriate commands to the motors. For this purpose, varying PWM signals are given to MOTOR_PIN_1 and MOTOR_PIN_2. To set the direction of the motors, we call digitalWrite(MOTOR_PIN_1, LOW) and digitalWrite(MOTOR_PIN_2, LOW).

The radio.stopListening method sets the chip select pin to LOW and flushes the RX and TX buffers of the nRF24L01 module. Similarly, the radio.startListening method also flushes the RX and TX buffers and sets the value of the chip select pin to HIGH in order to receive the next motor_value data.

The explanation of the serialEvent callback function can found in earlier chapters. So, there is no need for a duplicate explanation.

Now, we have built our Click-to-Go Robot! It's time to build the rest!

Building the vision application

We have built our robot in the previous sections and it is time to build the vision application as planned in the first section of this chapter. Before getting started, let's draw the physical scheme of our vision controller, as shown here:

As you can see from the picture, we use a second Arduino Uno R3 to communicate with the Arduino in the robot. Instead of this second Arduino, it is possible to use an FTDI converter, which is connected to the RF transceiver modem. But, we preferred the Arduino as it is the focus of this book. A webcam is also connected to the laptop over a USB interface. Our vision controller application will include a serial communication module to communicate with the robot over the RF transceiver. Instead of RF communication, Bluetooth classic, BLE, or Zigbee (for example, Xbee) can be used. If you want to establish a direct connection with the robot from a laptop without an external circuit, BLE would be a good choice. We already discussed all of these communication options in *Chapter 7, Communicating with Arduino Using OpenCV*.

The vision controller application was developed with Visual Studio 2012 on Windows 7. We won't repeat here how to create an OpenCV project with Visual Studio because it was discussed in the previous chapters.

We have many alternatives for serial communication. We have used Arduino's serial communication example for Windows because it is easy to implement and integrate.

> You can find more information about Windows serial interfacing on Arduino's webpage at http://playground.arduino.cc/ Interfacing/CPPWindows.

As stated before, we preferred a blob analysis-based processing technique for this application. To be able to apply blob analysis, we have used cvBlobsLib, which is an open source library.

> The latest version of the cvBlobsLib library and the documentation can be downloaded from http://sourceforge.net/projects/ cvblobslib/.

Building a vision controller and communications

Before getting started with the code, you should download the source files from https://github.com/ozenozkaya/click_to_go_robot_cv.

> The source codes for this book are also available at the Packt Publishing website (www.packtpub.com).

Once you get the source files, you should add all the files to your OpenCV project in Visual Studio. Once you add the source files, your project tree should look similar to this screenshot:

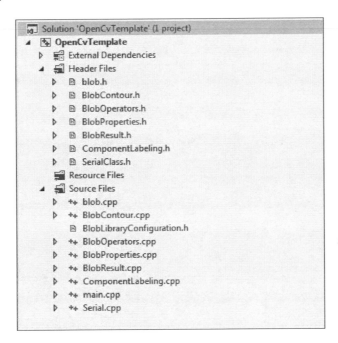

You can now compile the project. But, before running in, you should connect your Arduino with BLE to your computer or laptop over a USB port. Windows will load the Arduino USB driver and it will see the Arduino as a COM port device. Before getting started you should check the Arduino COM port and change the line in the `main.cpp` file to the Arduino COM port in your setup:

```
Serial* SP = new Serial("\\\\.\\COM18");
```

Check the COM port that the Arduino is connected to, and change the code to match. If the Arduino is attached to the `COM42` port in your computer or laptop, you should change the preceding line as follows:

```
Serial* SP = new Serial("\\\\.\\COM42");
```

This will create a serial port object with the correct COM port. Before explaining the code, you can run it if you click on any point in the window that is not on the robot, and you should see a screen similar to the following:

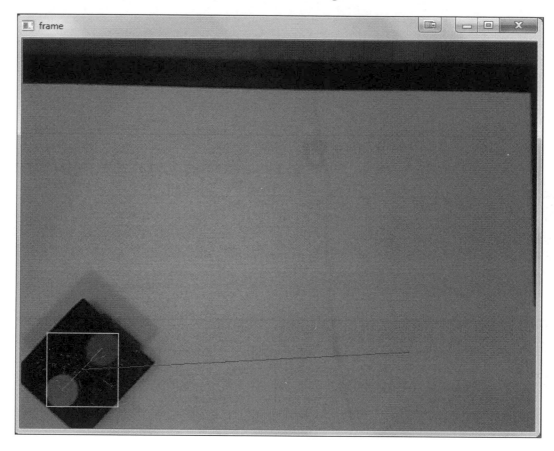

You can see that our vision controller detects the robot and draws a green bounding box around the circles. The values of the intervals in redFilter and blueFilter might change in your setup, and you should change them if you need to. The red line is the line that connects the centers of the red and blue circles. You can see that the orientation of the red line indicates the orientation of the robot. Do not forget that the red circle is the head of the robot. Once you click on any point, you'll see the blue line, which is the path from the center of the robot to the destination point. After that, the robot will turn towards the destination point and go forward to reach it. Once it reaches the destination point, the robot will stop. This can be seen in the following frames, shown here:

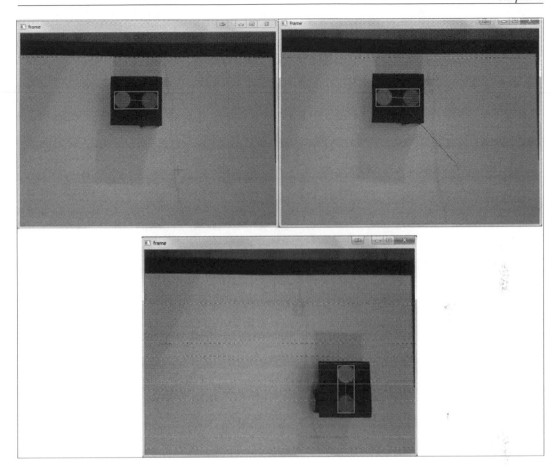

Once we understand the behavior we can start to explain the application code. We won't put the codes here because the application codes are too long,. You should download the codes from GitHub (https://github.com/ozenozkaya/click_to_go_robot_cv) and then you can find the main.cpp file.

Now, let's explain the code! We'll only explain main.cpp because the other files have documentation on the project pages, as shown in the links in the previous section. We'll also skip the header files because they were discussed in previous chapters.

At the beginning of the code, you can see the various #define statements:

```
#define PI 3.14159265
#define MAX_BLUR_KERNEL_LENGTH  (9)
```

The first definition is the PI number, which is used in angle calculation. In the next line, the maximum kernel length for blurring is defined as 9 because this filter size is sufficient for us. Here is the code snippet:

```
void robot_mouse_callback( int event, int x, int y, int flags,
void* param );
```

In the preceding code section, the mouse callback method prototype is declared. We need this function because the user will click on the window to set a destination point for the robot. We'll explain the function itself later.

You'll see the redFilter and the blueFilter functions, which are built with the OpenCV inRange function, as shown here:

```
inRange(src, Scalar(0, 0, 50), Scalar(35, 30, 160), red_only);
```

Since we'll apply two separate color filters for the red and blue circles, we have these two functions.

Now, let's go through the main function. You will see the serial port initializations there.

```
Serial* SP = new Serial("\\\\.\\COM18");     // adjust as needed
if (SP->IsConnected())
    printf("We're connected to serial controller\r\n");
else
{
    printf("Serial connect error\r\n");
    return -1;
}
SP->WriteData("Stop!",strlen("Stop!"));
```

A Serial class object pointer SP is created for the COM18 port. You have already changed the COM port string in this line to fit your setup. We then check if the serial port connection to the Arduino has been established. If there is a connection error, the program returns with the error code minus one:

```
VideoCapture cap(0);
    if(!cap.isOpened())
        return -1;
```

In the code in the preceding section, we opened a video capture and checked if it is opened. If you have multiple cameras attached to your computer, you can change the index to 0 if you need to:

```
int erosion_size = 1;
Mat element = getStructuringElement( MORPH_ELLIPSE,
```

The erosion/dilation kernel is created with the preceding code. You should be familiar with this function as we discussed it in detail in *Chapter 4, Filtering Data with OpenCV*. As you see, we are combining all the information from the previous chapters. The next step is reading an initial frame from the video capture:

```
Mat frame;
cap >> frame;
if(frame.data == NULL)
{
    printf("Frame is NULL!\r\n");
    return -1;
}
```

The initialization is now finished. You will see the main loop in the next line. We read the new frame as we did in the preceding code. Then we register a mouse callback to handle the mouse click operations, which is shown here:

```
cvSetMouseCallback("frame", robot_mouse_callback, (void*)&frame);
```

The cvSetMouseCallback function will register the robot_mouse_callback function for the window named frame and it will pass the latest image frame as a parameter to the callback function.

We then apply a Gaussian blur to the input frame, as shown here:

```
for (int i = 1; i < MAX_BLUR_KERNEL_LENGTH; i = i + 2 )
{
    GaussianBlur( frame, frame, Size( i, i ), 0, 0 );
}
```

In the next section of the code, we apply color filters of red and blue to the frame separately and we get red and blue image masks:

```
Mat blueImg = blueFilter(frame);
erode(blueImg,blueImg,element);
dilate( blueImg, blueImg, element );


Mat redImg = redFilter(frame);
erode(redImg,redImg,element);
dilate( redImg, redImg, element );
```

Then we start the blob analysis, in the following code:

```
CBlobResult blobs;
IplImage* img = new IplImage(redImg);
blobs = CBlobResult( img, NULL, 0 );
blobs.Filter( blobs, B_INCLUDE, CBlobGetArea(), B_GREATER, 200 );
```

This code section creates a CBlobResult object called as blobs. IplImage is a native image representation type which is originally taken from the Intel Image Processing library. Since cvBlobsLib uses IplImage instead of Mat, we create a new IplImage pointer img, which is constructed from a red image mask. Then we apply erosion and dilation to remove small details in the image. The blob analysis is done. The next line filters the blobs according to their area. Any blob which has an area smaller than 200 (pixel x pixel) will be filtered.

If you have multiple blobs, you can compare the properties of the blobs. On the other hand, the only red part in the scene is the red circle in our application. The same is valid for the blue circle. Because of this, we only get one blob with a zero index. Here is the remaining code:

```
CBlob currentBlob = blobs.GetBlob(0);
redBlobBoundingBox = currentBlob.GetBoundingBox();
rx = currentBlob.MinX() + (redBlobBoundingBox.width/2);
ry = currentBlob.MinY() + (redBlobBoundingBox.height/2);
```

As you can see from the preceding code section, we get the blob reference and we get the blob bounding box. The variable set (rx, ry) will give the center point of the red circle. The same operations are also applied for the blue circle. The resulting center points of the blue blob are bx and by:

```
line(frame,Point(rx,ry),Point(bx,by),Scalar(0,0,255));
```

The line function draws lines and we draw a red line from the center of the red circle to the center of the blue circle. Then, the robot orientation angle in degrees is calculated by using the angle of the red line:

```
robot_angle = -atan2(ry - by , rx - bx ) * 180 / PI;
```

Then we have combined the red and blue circle masks to get the image of the robot. We assumed that the bounding box of the two circles can represent the bounding box of the robot. This assumption works very well in practice. Here is the remaining code snippet:

```
Mat robot;
add(redImg,blueImg,robot);
img = new IplImage(robot);
blobs = CBlobResult( img, NULL, 0 );
blobs.Filter( blobs, B_INCLUDE, CBlobGetArea(), B_GREATER, 200 );
```

As you can see from the preceding code section, a new blob analysis is applied to the new robot matrix. An area filter is again applied to remove the small blobs, if there are any. Here is the remaining code snippet:

```
robot_center_x = (robot_min_x + robot_max_x)/2;
robot_center_y = (robot_min_y + robot_max_y)/2;
rectangle(frame,Point(robot_min_x,robot_min_y),Point(robot_max_x,r
obot_max_y),Scalar(0,255,0));
```

The center points and the bounding box of the robot are calculated and a green rectangle is drawn to indicate the robot.

The next part of the `main` function implements a simple path plan if there are any destination points. This simple approach is useful but many other approaches are also possible for tackling this problem. We won't go further into this issue because path planning is not the focus of this book. Before explaining this part, let's jump to the place where the destination is set:

```
void robot_mouse_callback( int event, int x, int y, int flags,
void* param ){
    Mat* image = (Mat*) param;

switch( event ){
    case CV_EVENT_MOUSEMOVE:
        break;
    case CV_EVENT_LBUTTONDOWN:
        printf("Clicked to x=%d, y=%d\r\n",x,y);
        printf("Robot angle = %f degree\r\n", robot_angle);
        is_destination_available = true;
        destination_x = x;
        destination_y = y;
        destination_angle = -atan2(destination_y - robot_center_y
, destination_x - robot_center_x ) * 180 / PI;
        printf("Destination angle = %f degree\r\n",
destination_angle);
        break;

    case CV_EVENT_LBUTTONUP:

        break;
    default:
        break;
    }
}
```

Once a mouse click occurs, the `is_destination_available` flag is set and the destination point is saved. In the next line, the destination angle is calculated by using the angle of the line starting from the center of the robot to the destination point.

Now, let's go back to the `main` function. Once a destination is available, the vision controller tries to match the angle of the robot to the destination angle by sending the `turn left` or `turn right` commands to the robot. `Right!` is used to turn the robot to the right and `Left!` is used to turn the robot to the left. Once orientation is matched with a maximum distance of 10 degrees, the vision controller sends a `Go!` command to the robot and the robot goes straight to reach the destination:

```
if(is_destination_available)
{
line(frame,
Point(robot_center_x,robot_center_y),Point(destination_x,
destination_y),Scalar(255,0,0));

bool is_rotation_required=true;
if(destination_angle>robot_angle)
{
    float diff = destination_angle - robot_angle;
    if(diff > 10.0)
    {
        SP->WriteData("Left!",strlen("Left!"));
        is_rotation_required = true;
    }
    else
    {
        is_rotation_required = false;
    }
}
else
{
    float diff =   robot_angle - destination_angle;
    if(diff > 10.0)
    {
        SP->WriteData("Right!",strlen("Right!"));
        is_rotation_required = true;
    }
    else
    {
```

```
                is_rotation_required = false;
        }
    }

    if(is_rotation_required == false)
    {
        int x_diff = (robot_center_x - destination_x);
        int y_diff = (robot_center_y - destination_y);
        int distance = sqrt( (x_diff*x_diff) + (y_diff*y_diff) );

        if(distance > 50)
        {
            SP->WriteData("Go!",strlen("Go!"));
        }
        else
        {
            SP->WriteData("Stop!",strlen("Stop!"));
            is_destination_available = false;
        }
    }
```

As you can see from the preceding code section, the robot tries to reach the destination with a tolerance of 50 pixels. If the distance is less than 50 pixels, the robot assumes the destination has been reached. This threshold can be changed as you wish. As you can see, the resolution of the camera and the distance from the robot affect image processing significantly. Here, we can only measure destinations in pixels. These measurements can be translated into inches or centimeters, but the conversion depends on the resolution of the camera, its field of view, and the distance from the object. Please change any of these parameters in your setup to see the effects.

The image frame is displayed in each loop with a 60 ms delay:

```
imshow("frame",frame);
if(waitKey(60) >= 0) break;
If program stops, vision controller sends a "Stop!" command to
stop the movements of the robot.
SP->WriteData("Stop!",strlen("Stop!"));
return 0;
```

Summary

We have combined everything we have learned up to now and built an all-in-one application. By designing and building the *Click-to-Go robot* from scratch you have embraced the concepts discussed in previous chapters. You can see that the vision approach used in this book works very well, even for complex applications. You now know how to divide a computer vision application into small pieces, how to design and implement each design step, and how to efficiently use the tools you have.

You can apply what you have learned from this book to different applications, whereby you will enhance your knowledge on computer vision. We hope that you enjoyed reading this book. And never forget that even the sky won't be the limit for you. Explore and happy learning.

Index

R

Radio Frequency (RF)
  about 131, 163
  URL 132
recognition 8
region 100
robot
  building 163
  electronics, building 165, 166
  mechanics, building 164-165
  robot controller,
      building 168-177
rotations per minute (rpm) 145
RX (receive) 117
RXTX libraries, for multiple platforms
  URL 133
RXTX library files
  URL 134
RXTX library webpage
  URL 133

S

Scale Invariant Feature Transform. *See* **SIFT**
sensor data acquisition
  Arduino environment, setting up 47
  Arduino, using 47
sensors
  fundamentals 48
  noises, dealing with 50
  sampling theorem 49
  types 48
Serial Peripheral Interface (SPI) 48, 115
servo motors
  driving 148-151
sharpening 57-59
SIFT
  about 97
  features 97
smoothing 57, 58
Sobel filter
  about 71, 72
  URL, for documentation 72

spatial domain filtering
  about 56, 57
  sharpening 58, 59
  smoothing 57, 58
Speeded Up Robust Features. *See* **SURF**
stepper motors
  driving 145-148
support vector machine (SVM)
  URL 113
  using 111-113
SURF
  about 99
  URL 99

T

temperature sensor
  data, reading from 50-54
template matching 103
TFT screens
  about 154
  URL 154
  using 154-158
thin-film transistor (TFT) 151
tracking 102
TX (transmit) 117

U

Universal Serial Bus (USB) 116
Universal Synchronous and Asynchronous
      Receiver/Transmitter (USART) 48

V

Virtual COM Port (VCP) 116
vision application
  building 177, 178
  communications, building 178-187
  vision controller, building 178-187
vision-enabled robot
  building 159-162

W

webcam
  used, for taking snapshot 37, 38
  video stream, obtaining from 38, 39
Windows
  OpenCV, installing on 21, 22
wired communications
  about 117
  communicating, via Ethernet 127, 128
  communicating, via serial port 124-127
  communicating, via USB 117-123

wireless communications
  about 128
  communicating, via Bluetooth
    Low Energy 128, 129
  communicating, via RF 131, 132
  communicating, via Wi-Fi 130, 131
  communicating, via ZigBee 130

X

Xcode
  OpenCV, using 21
  URL 20

Thank you for buying
Arduino Computer Vision Programming

About Packt Publishing

Packt, pronounced 'packed', published its first book, *Mastering phpMyAdmin for Effective MySQL Management*, in April 2004, and subsequently continued to specialize in publishing highly focused books on specific technologies and solutions.

Our books and publications share the experiences of your fellow IT professionals in adapting and customizing today's systems, applications, and frameworks. Our solution-based books give you the knowledge and power to customize the software and technologies you're using to get the job done. Packt books are more specific and less general than the IT books you have seen in the past. Our unique business model allows us to bring you more focused information, giving you more of what you need to know, and less of what you don't.

Packt is a modern yet unique publishing company that focuses on producing quality, cutting-edge books for communities of developers, administrators, and newbies alike. For more information, please visit our website at www.packtpub.com.

About Packt Open Source

In 2010, Packt launched two new brands, Packt Open Source and Packt Enterprise, in order to continue its focus on specialization. This book is part of the Packt Open Source brand, home to books published on software built around open source licenses, and offering information to anybody from advanced developers to budding web designers. The Open Source brand also runs Packt's Open Source Royalty Scheme, by which Packt gives a royalty to each open source project about whose software a book is sold.

Writing for Packt

We welcome all inquiries from people who are interested in authoring. Book proposals should be sent to author@packtpub.com. If your book idea is still at an early stage and you would like to discuss it first before writing a formal book proposal, then please contact us; one of our commissioning editors will get in touch with you.

We're not just looking for published authors; if you have strong technical skills but no writing experience, our experienced editors can help you develop a writing career, or simply get some additional reward for your expertise.

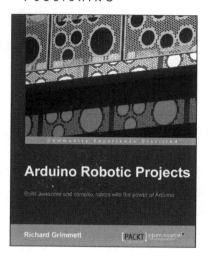

Arduino Robotic Projects

ISBN: 978-1-78398-982-9   Paperback: 240 pages

Build awesome and complex robots with the power of Arduino

1. Develop a series of exciting robots that can sail, go under water, and fly.

2. Simple, easy-to-understand instructions to program Arduino.

3. Effectively control the movements of all types of motors using Arduino.

4. Use sensors, GPS, and a magnetic compass to give your robot direction and make it lifelike.

OpenCV Computer Vision Application Programming Cookbook
Second Edition

ISBN: 978-1-78216-148-6   Paperback: 374 pages

Over 50 recipes to help you build computer vision applications in C++ using the OpenCV library

1. Master OpenCV, the open source library of the computer vision community.

2. Master fundamental concepts in computer vision and image processing.

3. Learn the important classes and functions of OpenCV with complete working examples applied on real images.

Please check **www.PacktPub.com** for information on our titles

Arduino Home Automation Projects

ISBN: 978-1-78398-606-4   Paperback: 132 pages

Automate your home using the powerful
Arduino platform

1. Interface home automation components
    with Arduino.

2. Automate your projects to communicate
    wirelessly using XBee, Bluetooth and WiFi.

3. Build seven exciting, instruction-based home
    automation projects with Arduino in no time.

Arduino Essentials

ISBN: 978-1-78439-856-9   Paperback: 206 pages

Enter the world of Arduino and its peripherals and
start creating interesting projects

1. Meet Arduino and its main components and
    understand how they work to use them in your
    real-world projects.

2. Assemble circuits using the most common
    electronic devices such as LEDs, switches,
    optocouplers, motors, and photocells and
    connect them to Arduino.

3. A Precise step-by-step guide to apply basic
    Arduino programming techniques in the
    C language.

Please check **www.PacktPub.com** for information on our titles

97018412R00124